amazing baby

amazing
baby

the amazing story of the
first two years of life

desmond morris

FIREFLY BOOKS

A FIREFLY BOOK

Published by Firefly Books Ltd. 2008

First printing

Publisher Cataloging-in-Publication Data (U.S.)

Morris, Desmond.
    Amazing baby : the amazing story of the first two years of life /
Desmond Morris.
[192] p. : col. photos. ; cm.
Includes index.
Summary: A discovery tour through a baby's first two years of life;
from conception, to development in the womb, to birth and to early
development.
ISBN-13: 978-1-55407-419-8
ISBN-10: 1-55407-419-3
1. Infants. 2. Infants — Development. I. Title.
305.232 dc22   HQ774.M665Am 2008

Library and Archives Canada Cataloguing in Publication

Morris, Desmond
    Amazing baby : the amazing story of the first two years of life /
Desmond Morris.
Includes index.
ISBN-13: 978-1-55407-419-8
ISBN-10: 1-55407-419-3
    1. Infants — Development. 2. Fetus — Development. I. Title.
HQ774.M664 2008   305.232   C2008-902823-6

Published in the United States by
Firefly Books (U.S.) Inc.
P.O. Box 1338, Ellicott Station
Buffalo, New York 14205

Published in Canada by
Firefly Books Ltd.
66 Leek Crescent
Richmond Hill, Ontario L4B 1H1

Developed by Hamlyn, a division of Octopus Publishing Group Ltd
2–4 Heron Quays, London E14 4JP
Executive editor: Jane McIntosh
Senior editor: Fiona Robertson
Deputy creative director: Karen Sawyer
Designer: Janis Utton
Illustrator: Kevin Jones Associates
Picture research manager: Giulia Hetherington
Picture researcher: Sally Claxton
Production manager: Ian Paton

Printed in China

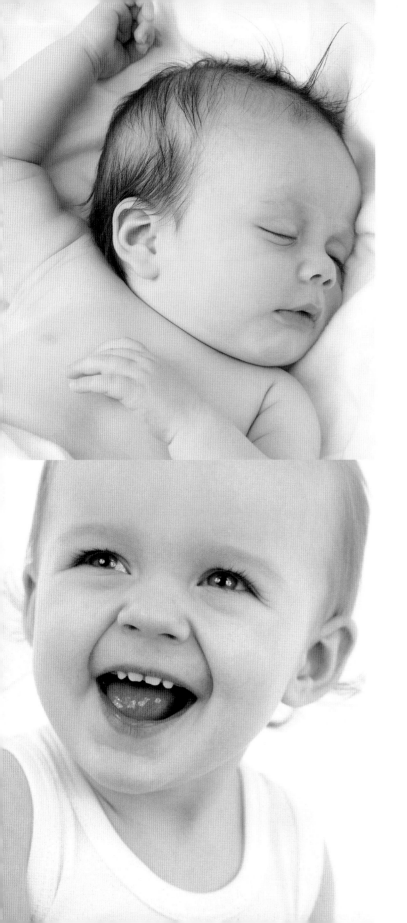

contents

foreword

The human baby is truly amazing and this book is a celebration of that fact. Many baby books have been written from the point of view of the parent, offering advice on how to look after an infant, but this one is different. Instead of giving advice, it sets out to paint an accurate portrait of the first two years of human life, as seen from the child's point of view. Armed with this information it is then up to the parent to decide how best to care for a little one – from the day of his birth, when he arrives small, vulnerable and wordless, to the day he celebrates his second birthday, already walking, talking and challenging the world.

Perhaps the most astonishing fact about a baby is that, during the nine months between conception and birth, his weight increases by a staggering 3,000 million times. As soon as he is born, this meteoric growth rate slows down dramatically, so that between birth and the end of his second year an infant will have only quadrupled in size. This may seem like an impressive growth to parents, but it is nothing compared to the astonishing development that takes place inside the womb.

an evolutionary journey

The unfolding of a baby's qualities and abilities is a complex story. His tiny body has the backing of a million years of human evolution, helping different features to develop in a special sequence. All the new baby needs now is a friendly environment in which this can happen.

Evolution has armed the infant with an irresistible appeal that ensures his parents care for him, tend him, feed him and keep him clean and warm. Even the most sophisticated adults are transformed into doting protectors when faced with the helpless bundle in their arms, staring up at them with big, questioning eyes. Bearing in mind the amount of time and effort that goes into looking after a newborn, this is just as well.

a parent's role

For human beings the parental burden is huge, lasting nearly two decades for each child, but it can also be a source of intense joy. And babies are more than just babies. They also happen to be our only certain form of immortality, in the sense that they carry on our genetic line, ensuring that our genes do not die out when we ourselves come to the end of our own lives.

The importance of a baby's first two years of life cannot be overestimated. Many of the qualities he acquires during this sensitive period mark him for life. A toddler who is provided with a rich, varied, exciting environment in which he is encouraged to start exploring, and who is treated lovingly by dependable parents, stands the very best chance of acquiring a sense of confident curiosity, creative wonder and active intelligence in later life. Nestling inside his fragile head, a newborn baby has the genetically inherited equipment that is needed for this development. All his parents have to do is to offer him the setting in which this equipment can whirr into action, allowing him to fulfill his human potential. The secret is simply to let natural loving feelings express themselves – a child needs a lot of love and complete trust in the reliability of his protectors if he is to flourish.

every child is unique

Although this book looks at the common features possessed by all babies during the first two years of their lives, it must never be forgotten that every baby is unique. Each child has a DNA that is shared by no one else on the planet – even identical twins are born with different sets of fingerprints. It is the combination of a baby's genetic makeup with her specific upbringing and environment that shapes the adult individual into which she grows.

physical variations

Parents should always bear in mind that for every child who grows and acquires skills at a particular speed, there will be another who is much slower and another who is much faster. For every child of a particular weight, there will be another who is heavier and another who is lighter. Sometimes the variations between the extremes are enormous: the heaviest birth weight ever recorded for a human baby is over 35 times as much as the lightest weight recorded. The timings for developmental milestones given in this book can therefore only be approximate.

emergence of personality

Babies also show considerable variations in personality – variations that are inborn and that are not dependent on environmental differences. Almost all parents who have had several children will tell you that, to their surprise, their little ones have turned out to have strikingly different personalities. One will be quiet and placid, another lively and sociable, another careful and industrious. One will be the helpful one, another the difficult one and yet another the clever one. And even if the children have all been brought up in much the same way and in a similar domestic environment, they will still exhibit these clear differences.

the role of DNA

Variations in appearance and personality are reminders of the fact that each of us has a unique DNA and is genetically different from every other one of the 6 billion human beings who walk the earth today. It is these variations that make us so different from the production-line humanoid robots of science-fiction nightmare. Our differences are what make life on this small planet of ours so enjoyable. But although there are thousands of tiny details in which we differ from one another, there are thousands more that make us very similar. And it is these similarities, rather than the differences, that this book is presenting.

the role of the environment

In addition to the inborn characteristics of each new baby, additional influences come from the baby's environment, especially the home in which she starts to grow up. All babies are genetically programmed to develop at more or less the same rate, but a happy home life may speed up some of these processes, while a hostile or unchallenging one may slow them down. The mental capacities of a baby who grows up in a highly stimulating world may end up being much greater than if she had been born into a harsh or boring environment.

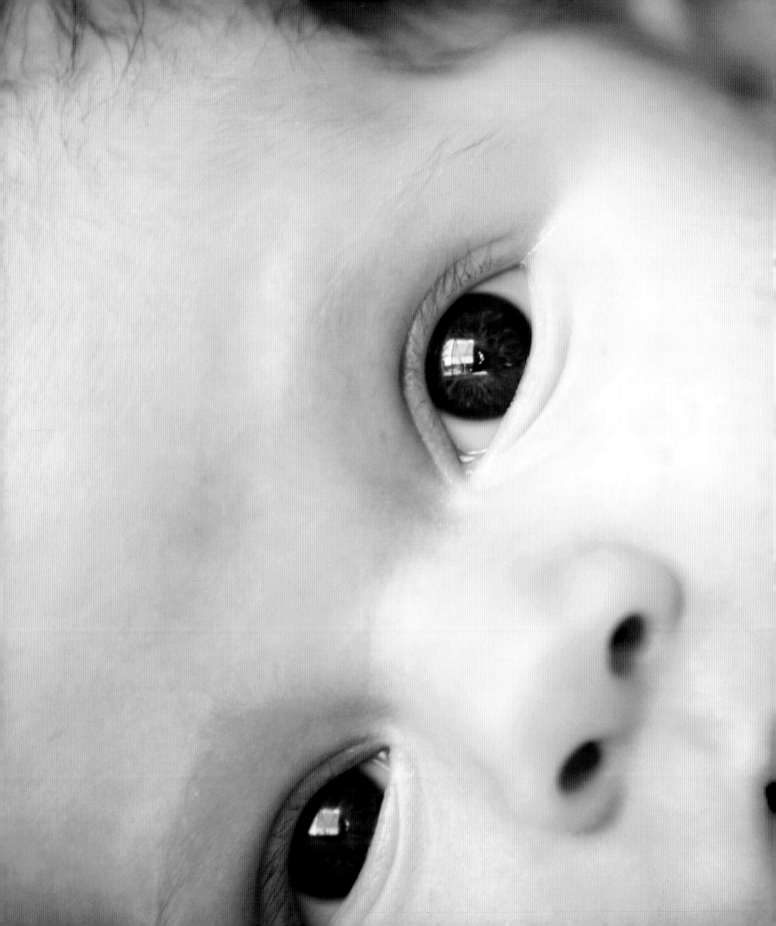

a new baby

birth

The moment of birth comes as a great shock to a baby. Life inside the womb is cozy – warm, dark, quiet, soft, liquid and all embracing. Suddenly, after some brutal squeezing, all of that comforting environment vanishes. Now there is bright light, noise, hard surfaces, loss of body contact and this strange sensation of being surrounded, not by liquid, but by air. No wonder the baby lets out a cry of panic.

new surroundings

The environment into which a baby is born is traditionally one of hospital efficiency, where it is deemed imperative for the procedure to be swift and hygienic. As rapidly as possible, the medical team cut and clamp the umbilical cord and examine the baby for defects. They then weigh him, wash him and wrap him in a snug blanket. For the vast majority of babies, who are born fit and healthy, the mood could easily be more relaxed and calm and this would lessen the shock of birth.

gently does it

Observations of newborn babies reveal that they are far less traumatized by the drama of being born if they are greeted, not by noise and excitement, but by peace and quiet, and in a room with soft lighting. Bright light may be needed for the birth itself, but once the baby has arrived safely, dimming the lights allows his eyes to adapt more gradually to the new demands put upon them.

Allowing a newborn baby to remain in close contact with his mother's body, instead of being picked up and examined right away by other hands, also greatly reduces his sense of panic at the loss of soft body contact. Placed on his mother's stomach so that she herself can embrace him, a baby will sense a continuity of the warm body intimacy he has been enjoying for the past nine months. It is no accident that the umbilical cord is of just the right length – approximately 20 inches (50 cm) – to make this possible while the baby is still attached to the placenta.

Babies treated in this more relaxed way demonstrate far less panic. There is no prolonged screaming or grimacing. The infant lies quietly on his mother's body, as he slowly recovers from his difficult journey. As far as the baby is concerned, there is no urgency at this point. His cord is still active and continues to beat for several minutes after the delivery is complete. During this time he starts to breathe the air, with his little lungs slowly taking over from the activity of the cord. This switch, if not interfered with, is a gradual one. At the same time, he receives the last drop of blood available to him from the cord supply.

early intimacy

Those assisting at the birth are probably impatient to get a baby washed, weighed and wrapped up but, if they wait a little while, both mother and baby will have time to experience the first sensations of bonding. The baby soon succumbs to the deep sleep of recovery, but for a while immediately after birth he is wide awake and, if allowed to do so, spends a great deal of time staring up at his mother as she looks down at him. In an ideal world, neither should be robbed of these intimate moments.

Eventually, the time comes for the baby's cord to be cut, and for him to be taken away for cleaning, weighing and wrapping up. If he has experienced this quiet time in his mother's arms he finds this interruption far less stressful. Once clean, a baby should be returned to his mother's arms and the two should be separated as little as possible during the first few days of his new life.

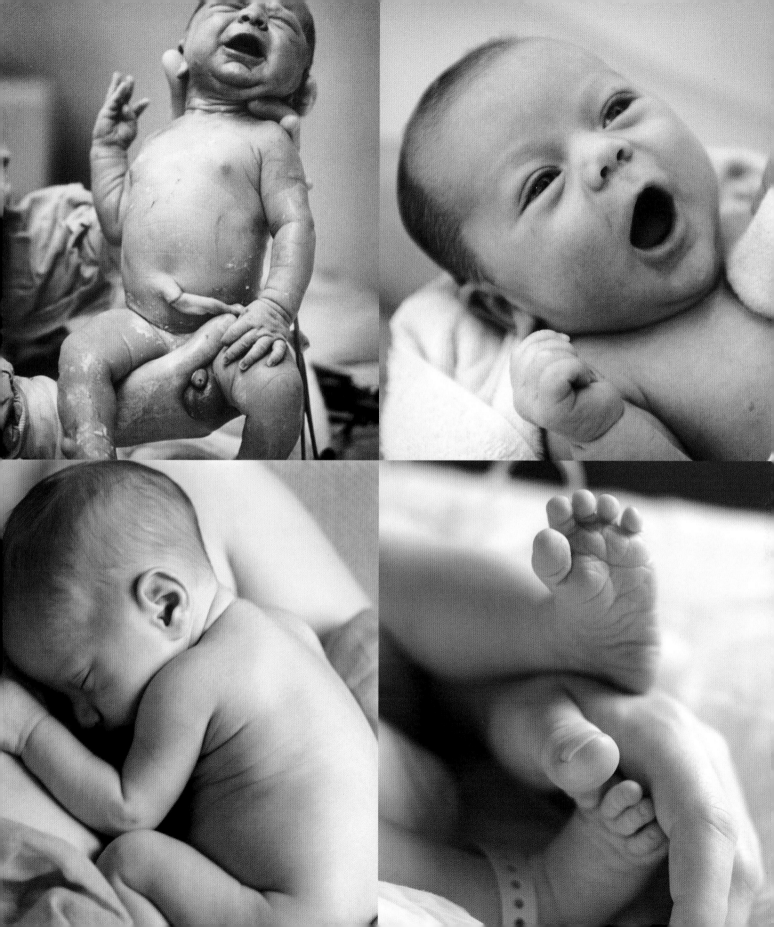

the newborn body

During her first few days of life outside the womb, a baby's body may seem less than perfect, but the early blemishes soon disappear. She has, after all, been lying curled up inside the womb for months and has just undergone the physical trauma of being squeezed, with some difficulty, through the birth canal: it is not surprising that she shows a few signs of these past experiences in her first days of freedom.

initial imperfections

A newborn baby's skin may show signs of her recent ordeal. These include red marks on the head and neck, sometimes referred to as "stork bites," which are tiny blood vessels visible through the skin. There may also be spots, rashes and peeling skin. All of these marks start to disappear as the body recovers from the rough treatment of being born and the baby adapts to life outside the womb. In the immediate period after birth, parents may see what is known as the "harlequin" effect. One half of the baby's body turns a deep red, while the other remains pale. This harmless reaction is caused by variations in the diameter of the blood vessels and is usually triggered by a change in position or temperature. Mottling of the skin is also common, owing to the immaturity of the circulatory system.

Eyelids may be puffy from the pressure exerted on them during birth but these, too, soon recover. Sometimes a baby may appear to have a squint during her earliest weeks, but this nearly always disappears during the first few months.

As she does not have to squeeze through the narrow birth canal, a baby arriving by cesarean delivery will be unblemished and her skull will not be distorted. However, a cesarean is a major operation – not without risk to mother and baby – and should only be performed for medical reasons. Research has shown that cesarean babies are more likely to have breathing difficulties, as it is thought they may miss out on important hormonal and physiological changes that occur during labor.

belly button

Shortly after birth the umbilical cord is clamped and cut, close to the navel. The piece that remains attached to the baby's belly soon starts to dry up naturally. This happens much faster if the stump is exposed to the air. Once dry and withered, the clamp is removed and the remaining piece of cord drops off of its own accord, usually within about 10 days, leaving behind a clean navel, or "belly button." It may take a little longer – anything up to three weeks – before it detaches itself, but it is important to let nature take its course. When it does finally happen there may be a few drops of blood, but these soon dry up. The resulting belly button may be convex (an "outie") or concave (an "innie") – both are completely normal.

breasts and genitals

In four or five out of every 100 newborn babies, there is a discharge of milk from the nipples. This is caused by the stimulation of the baby's breasts by unusually high levels of

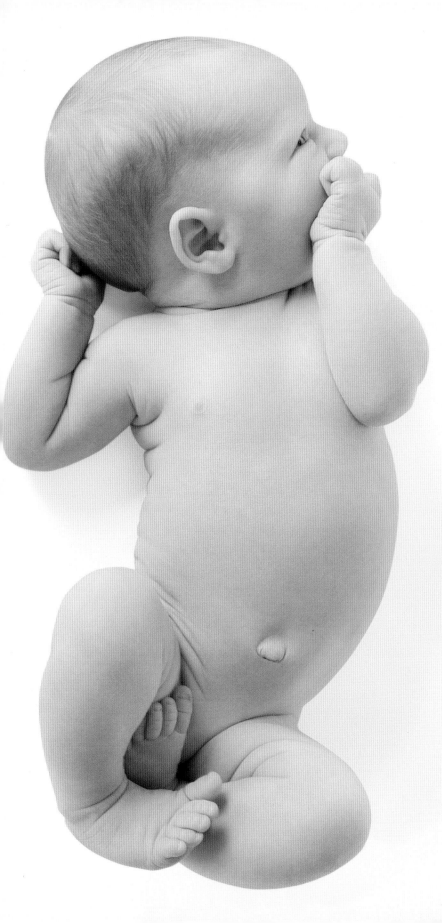

the mother's hormones that leak across the placenta during pregnancy and remain in the baby's system during her earliest days following birth. This discharge of milk is never seen in premature babies, only in those that reach full term. When it occurs, there is a small swelling, or breast nodule, underneath the nipple. Best left untouched, this may appear in both girl and boy babies and disappears within a few weeks.

Again, because of the presence of the mother's hormones in the new baby's system for the first few weeks of life outside the womb, it is perfectly natural for both boys and girls to be born with disproportionately large genitals. This is especially true of the male scrotum.

body shape

At birth, a baby's arms and legs are unusually short. Her length, relative to the rest of the body, continues to increase until she is fully adult. A newborn baby's shoulders and hips are rather narrow. The head is proportionally huge, being one-quarter of the total body length, compared to only one-eighth of the total adult length. During the first week or so, instead of growing, a baby's weight may actually decrease by about 5 percent, but this is perfectly normal and is due to a reduced intake of fluids: it takes a while for the mother's milk to come in and the baby feeds on the more concentrated colostrum for the first few days. She returns to her birth weight within 10 to 20 days and shows a steady increase from then on.

a baby's head

At birth, a baby's head creates a problem for his mother. When prehistoric woman first stood up on hind legs and started to walk, her pelvis had to adapt to this new mode of vertical locomotion. This meant a more restricted birth canal and a more difficult delivery. If the fetal skull were broad and stiff, a baby's passage into the outside world would be too clumsy and painful. There needed to be, therefore, some kind of streamlining in order to ease a baby's headfirst journey from the womb.

a modified skull

At the time of his birth, a baby's skull is amazingly soft and pliable. Although later on it must act as a rigid, biological crash helmet, protecting the all-important brain, at this stage it is more concerned with the challenge of being squeezed through the mother's vaginal passage. The softness of the bones helps, but there is more. In addition to their pliability, these skull bones are divided up into a number of separate plates, each capable of overlapping slightly with others. This gives the baby's head a slimmer, more tapered shape as it passes down the tight birth canal. The baby's small, movable jaw aids this process further.

natural distortions

The wonderful flexibility of a newborn's skull can leave a baby looking a little battered, even lopsided, as he emerges into the outside world. These distortions are a natural part of the birth process and soon disappear. Within a few days, almost every baby has a perfectly shaped and symmetrical skull, the soft bony plates having gradually rearranged themselves. Even in the most extreme cases, where the delivery has been unusually difficult, the remolding of the baby's skull takes no more than a few weeks. This skull distortion is most conspicuous with first-time mothers. The passage through the canal becomes easier with each subsequent birth until, eventually, there is hardly any distortion at all.

Following birth, a baby's skull takes several months to harden and become the efficient, protective casing that his brain so badly needs. During this early phase, it is especially vulnerable to physical damage and the mother has to be careful to offer as much protection as she can.

soft spots

The bony plates of a baby's skull remain separate for a time after birth. Small gaps between them are covered by a tough, membranous tissue that is strong enough to resist all forms of damage except a sharp, direct blow. At six points on the head, however, these narrow gaps widen out to form "soft spots" called fontanelles.

The two main fontanelles are on top of the head. The anterior fontanelle is located at the top of the forehead; the posterior one is toward the back of the top of the head. The four remaining, minor, soft spots are paired. The front pair is situated on either side of the temples; the rear pair is on either side toward the back of the head. It is sometimes possible to see a baby's pulse beating through the main anterior fontanelle.

These soft spots gradually disappear as the bony plates spread outward toward one another. The plates eventually touch, forming wavy sutures where they meet. These connections become harder and stronger until the whole skull is welded together and the infant's "crash helmet" has been perfected. The time this takes varies from child to child, the quickest time being about four months; the longest about four years. In most cases, however, completion takes between 18 and 24 months.

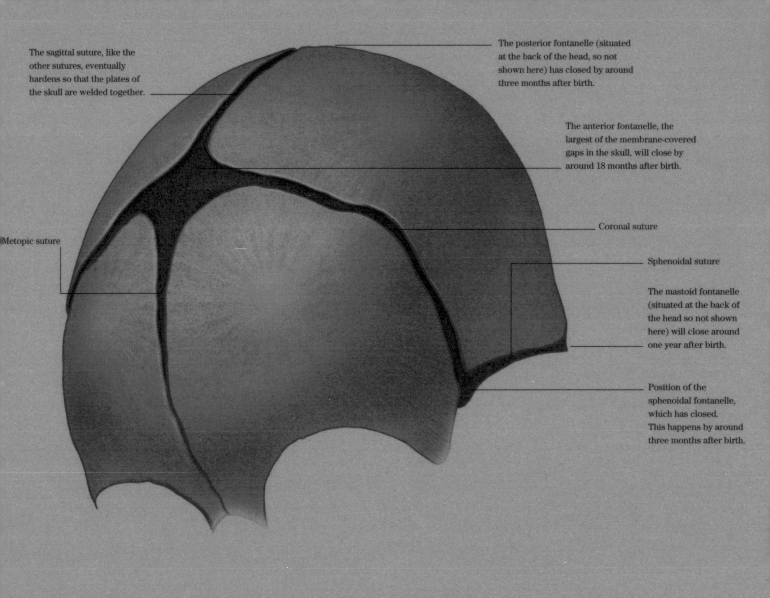

The sagittal suture, like the other sutures, eventually hardens so that the plates of the skull are welded together.

The posterior fontanelle (situated at the back of the head, so not shown here) has closed by around three months after birth.

The anterior fontanelle, the largest of the membrane-covered gaps in the skull, will close by around 18 months after birth.

Coronal suture

Sphenoidal suture

Metopic suture

The mastoid fontanelle (situated at the back of the head so not shown here) will close around one year after birth.

Position of the sphenoidal fontanelle, which has closed. This happens by around three months after birth.

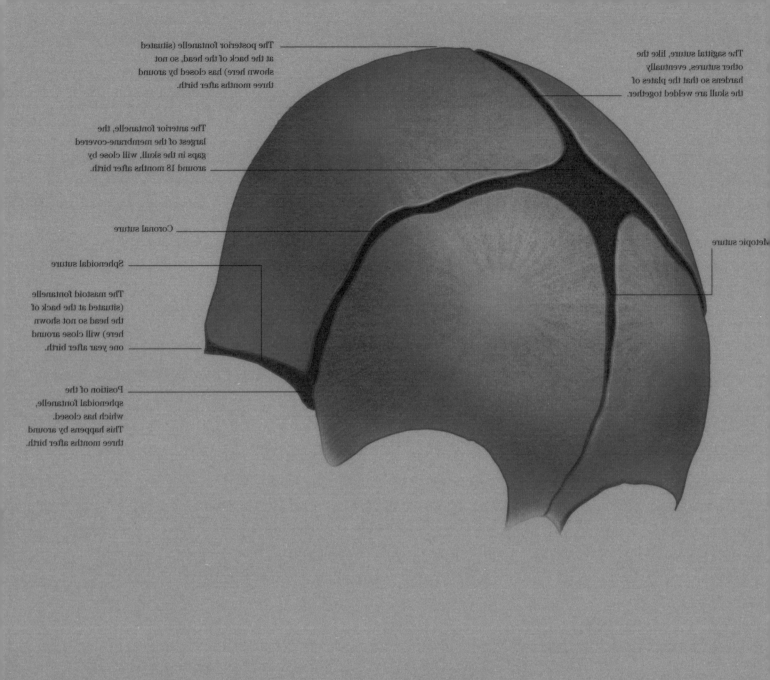

newborn skin

At birth, the surface of a baby's body is unusually vulnerable. With no fur to protect her, she must face the harshness of the outside world with a soft, naked skin that is all too easily damaged. Fortunately, there is nearly always some snug, warm clothing available in which to wrap a newborn and, in addition, nature provides its own special protective layer.

vernix

When born, a baby's skin is covered with a whitish grease called the vernix, a vital covering that acts as an essential aid during delivery. Without this skin lubricant, it would be almost impossible for a mother to squeeze her baby through the tight birth canal and into the outside world. The technical name for this "skin grease" is *vernix caseosa*, meaning literally "cheesy varnish." The reason it is whitish in color is that it is made up of a combination of flakes of skin shed by the fetus and the oily secretions of the sebaceous glands. These glands become especially active during the last few months of pregnancy, so that as the moment of birth approaches the fetus is covered all over in the slippery grease.

Following birth, the grease takes on a second role as a temporary insulating layer, helping the newborn to cope with the sudden drop in temperature as she finds herself rudely ejected from the cozy warmth of the womb. It also acts as a defensive barrier protecting the naked skin from minor infections during its first, vulnerable days in the outside world.

Some mothers leave the vernix in place until it falls away naturally by itself a few days later. Other mothers prefer to cleanse the skin as soon as possible, bathing the baby in warm water to remove the greasy layer. With the availability of modern hygiene, this premature loss of the protective vernix does little or no harm to a baby.

lanugo

In the final months of pregnancy, just before the vernix is produced, the hair follicles of the fetus become active. This sudden burst of activity leads to the copious oil secretion needed to create the lubricating vernix, but it also has the side effect of producing the rapid growth of a coat of fine downy hair, called the lanugo.

All babies have this woolly covering briefly when they are in the womb – it is a perfectly natural phase of the human life cycle – and in nearly all of them it disappears before birth, leaving only the greasy layer of oil for the moment of delivery. In a number of babies, however, the timing of the disappearance of the woolly coat is a little slow and is delayed until just after the birth. For some this means the whole body is covered, except for the palms of the hands and the soles of the feet. In others, only the face, shoulders and back are hairy. In others still, the lanugo is limited to the shoulders and back.

For some new mothers, this appearance of a woolly coat on the bodies of their newborn babies is a cause of some anxiety, but the lanugo usually vanishes within a few days and, at the very most, lasts for only a few weeks. The phenomenon is most commonly observed in premature babies who have been born at the earlier stage when all babies are developing the woolly coat, and it provides the newborn with an insulating layer in the absence of the vernix, which has not yet been produced.

body temperature

Human beings evolved in a warm climate where the control of body temperature was not a major problem. However, in spreading out across the globe, our ancestors encountered a whole range of extreme temperatures and had to devise ways of avoiding both chilling and overheating. Adults achieved this by using their intelligence – putting on thick clothing to keep warm or staying in the shade to keep cool. A newborn baby is not capable of making such adjustments, however, and must rely on the assistance of his parents.

correct temperature

All babies are vulnerable to temperature-control difficulties, and so it is important to have a picture of their ideal needs. Most crucial is the "neutral thermal temperature" – the level at which a baby can maintain his body temperature with the least amount of effort. For the naked newborn this is high, 90°F (32°C), but as soon as he is wrapped in snug clothing this drops to about 75°F (24°C). Within a few weeks of birth, a baby already starts to improve his body-temperature control and, if well clothed, can thrive at a slightly lower temperature of around 70°F (21°C).

a valuable secret weapon

A full-term, newborn baby does have one special heat-control mechanism: brown fat. At birth this makes up 5 percent of the baby's body and is located in the back, shoulders and neck. It liberates heat through a special chemical process if the baby's body starts to cool unduly. As the child grows and develops other ways of avoiding overcooling, the brown fat gradually transforms into ordinary white fat.

overheating

There are several factors that contribute to the chances of a baby overheating. If he feels too hot, he instinctively tries to kick off warm coverings. He may be able to push a blanket away with his legs, but tightly wrapped clothing poses more of a problem. Also, he is not yet capable of moving from a hot spot to a cooler one. If he cries as noisily as possible to alert his parents that something is amiss, this vigorous crying action only increases his body temperature even more, as the expenditure of energy involved raises his metabolism. If a parent arrives and imagines that the baby is crying because he is hungry, giving him warm milk only adds to his difficulties. For an adult, a hot drink causes sweating that can help to cool the body but, during the first two years of life, babies are poorly served with sweat glands. Furthermore, babies are exceptionally well served with generous layers of fat. These help to avoid overcooling and prevent heat loss, but they pose yet another problem for the overheated baby.

overcooling

Chilling is the other hazard that a baby must face. One of the problems with an overcooled baby is that it is not always easy to tell that he is in trouble because, if he is soundly asleep, his metabolism is slow to react to a serious drop in temperature. He only feels the cold, and reacts with loud cries, once he starts to wake up. So, by the time parents have been alerted, his body may already have begun chilling. An additional problem is that a baby is not yet able to shiver as a way of raising his body temperature.

premature babies

The risk of overcooling is even greater with premature babies, because they have not yet developed the brown fat layers that are so important in maintaining internal body heat. For this reason a baby can cool rapidly if the room temperature is not sufficiently high. The incubators used for premature babies are usually kept at about 90°F (32°C), but the thermostats have to be very accurate, as a rise of only a few more degrees could lead to serious overheating.

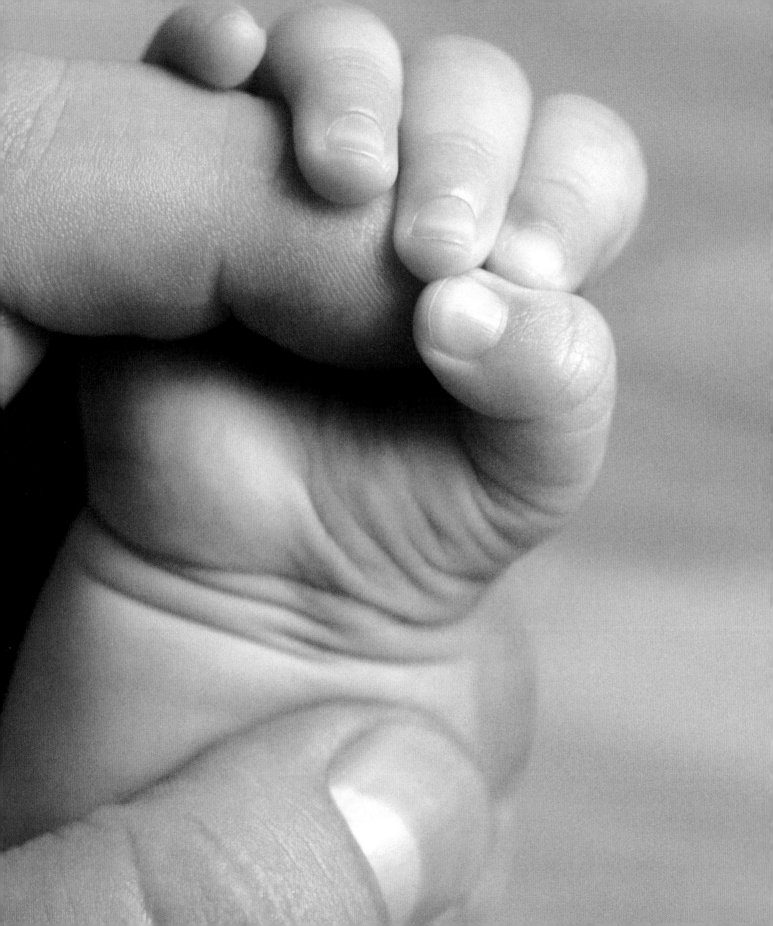

a baby's reflexes

A baby enters the world equipped with several automatic reflex actions that are controlled by the oldest part of the brain (the part that we share with lower forms of animal life). Although these fixed, primitive responses are present at birth, with one exception (the startle reflex), they soon start to fade and are later replaced by variable actions controlled by the more advanced parts of the brain. These reflexes act as a vivid reminder of our ancient past.

Moro reflex

When a newborn baby feels herself falling, she flings her arms out and opens her hands, spreading her fingers as wide as possible. She then brings her arms together, as if trying to embrace something. If her legs are free, she moves them in the same way. These are the actions that a baby ape would perform if he felt himself falling from his mother's body and was reaching out to cling on to her fur.

When the ancestral mother lost her coat of fur, this defensive action of the baby became meaningless and started to disappear. Today it remains in an incomplete form and is not carried through to the point where the baby actually tries to hang on to her mother's body. But, although the full clinging response has been lost, the relic gesture that remains is of some value because it alerts the mother to the fact that her baby is suddenly feeling unsafe and physically insecure.

The reflex also has a medical value because it enables a doctor to check a newborn baby's limb movements for any irregularities. When a healthy baby feels herself losing balance, she flings her limbs wide symmetrically. A doctor, by giving a newborn baby the sensation that she is falling, can check to make sure that the limbs on both sides of the body are opened to the same degree.

The Moro reflex does not last very long. All babies show it at birth and at the age of six weeks it is still present in 97 percent of them. The reflex then starts to fade in intensity and by two months may have disappeared altogether. More commonly, it does not vanish until the age of about three to four months, and by six months it will certainly have disappeared.

grasp reflex

Perhaps the most surprising of all the automatic responses displayed by the newborn baby is the grasp, or palmar, reflex. Another fascinating reminder of our evolutionary past, this reflex is reminiscent of a time before our ancestors lost their coat of fur, when their young clung to them tightly whenever they were carried. If a parent presses his forefingers into the palms of a newborn baby's hands, her tiny fingers respond by curling tightly and clinging on. Amazingly, if the parent then gently lifts the clasped forefingers, the baby, seemingly so helpless at this stage, holds on tight and finds herself being raised into the air. The grasp of a newborn baby is so strong that her whole body can hang in midair, with her bent fingers supporting her weight.

In some fast-growing babies this strange grasp reflex may disappear in less than a week, while in more typical babies it persists for several weeks, and in a few babies is still present after several months. By the age of six months, however, the grasp reflex vanishes altogether and there is a pause before the child reaches the next stage of efficient grasping – the voluntary grasping of the older baby who is starting to explore the world with her hands (see The hands, page 68).

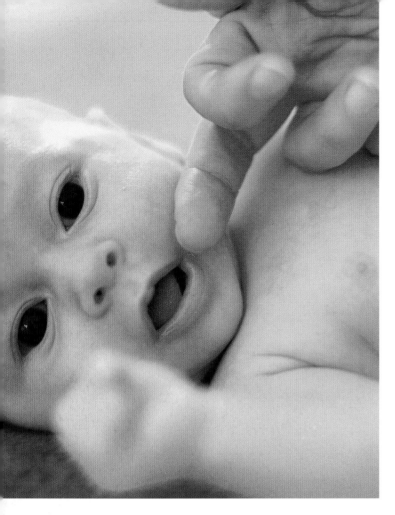

startle reflex

The startle response occurs when there is a loud and unexpected noise close to a baby's body. When this happens, her body stiffens, her shoulders hunch up and her arms move upward as if to protect her against some kind of attack. This is essentially a protective reaction and does not fade in a few months like other reflexes, but remains present throughout life, becoming stronger, if anything, on reaching adulthood.

plantar reflex

If a parent strokes the sole of a baby's foot from the heel to the toes, the baby reacts by flaring her toes up and turning her foot in. This is because the baby's nervous system is not yet fully developed. Between the ages of six to 18 months, the baby demonstrates the adult reaction of curling her toes down.

stepping reflex

When a baby is held upright and supported under her arms, she makes a stepping movement, as if trying to walk. This early reflex disappears by about three months.

rooting reflex

A crucially important automatic action that precedes feeding at the breast is the rooting reflex, where a baby turns her head toward any soft surface that makes gentle contact with her cheek. The nipple, the skin of the breast or even a lightly stroking finger will elicit such a reaction. The baby automatically turns her head in the direction of the stimulus and, at the same time, starts pouting her lips. If a mother softly touches her baby's cheek before trying to get her to suck on her nipple, it primes her for the next step – breast-feeding itself.

sucking reflex

All babies demonstrate the sucking reflex while still in the womb. After birth the action is stimulated by anything that touches the roof of a baby's mouth, and enables her to latch on to the nipple firmly enough to feed. The reflex makes way for a voluntary action by two to four months.

fencing reflex

This is also known as the tonic neck reflex and occurs when a baby is lying on her back. She turns her head to one side, extending the arm and leg on that side while flexing the arm and leg on the opposite side. This reflex may be present at birth or appear at around two months. It lasts approximately four months.

swimming

A newborn baby is physically helpless and spends much of his time curled up in the fetal position that is so familiar to him from his days inside the womb. His hands are clenched and his toes often curled. Unclothed he may wave his arms and legs around: if a finger or thumb happens to come close to his mouth he usually responds by sucking it. He is not yet capable of moving his body from A to B, unless he is in water.

swimming babies

One of the most astonishing discoveries of recent years has been the swimming ability of newborn babies. Tests have shown that, when a baby is lowered face down into warm water with a parental hand under his tummy, he shows no sign of panic but holds his breath automatically and floats happily in the water with his eyes fully open, gazing at the underwater scene. If, very gently, the supporting hand is removed, the baby starts making swimming movements with his limbs and sets off in the water.

So, although a newborn baby cannot move himself from place to place in the air, once he is allowed to float under the water he suddenly becomes remarkably mobile. He is capable, from birth and without any training, of performing well-organized, integrated swimming actions that propel him forward in a businesslike way. In other words, a baby can swim before he can walk. He can even swim before he can crawl. How can this be explained?

a return to the womb?

The obvious answer is that a baby feels at home in the water because he is pleasantly reminded of the liquid world in which he spent the last nine months. This explanation is flawed, however. A baby in the womb has not yet started to use his lungs but, when swimming in water, he is able to control his respiration. As soon as his mouth goes below the surface it automatically suppresses his breathing actions. Furthermore, there is no room to swim inside the womb and yet the baby in the water is using coordinated limb movements that move him along at a decent pace.

our aquatic origins

Newborn swimming is, therefore, a novel form of movement that we are seeing for the first time. It can only be explained as representing a primitive phase of our evolution, when our ancestors were far more aquatic than we are today. Sadly, it is only a relic action, a remnant of the past that does not last. By the time the baby has reached the age of three to four months it has vanished. From this time on, a baby panics if placed in the water and it is a long time before the swimming ability returns. When it does reappear it is completely different – a learned skill that has to be acquired gradually when the child is a few years older.

It should be stressed that allowing a newborn baby to swim, extraordinary as it is, must only be done with extreme caution. A baby can drown very easily in just an inch or two of water. Several adults need to be standing by, therefore, to "field" the baby as he swims. Also, the water needs to be much warmer than is usual for a typical swimming pool. And, most importantly, babies should not be allowed to swim in the heavily chlorinated pool water that is all too common these days. Because they keep their eyes wide open under the water, harsh chemicals could hurt their delicate surfaces. Together, these factors make baby-swimming far less common than it might otherwise be, which is a pity because it is just one more way in which mothers and fathers can learn that they are the parents of a truly amazing baby.

body systems

From the moment the umbilical cord is severed and the newborn baby takes her first breath, her internal organs start to work together efficiently as the key elements of an independent being. The first step is for the blood system to reorganize itself.

the prebreathing body

An unborn baby receives all her nutrition and oxygen through a vein in the umbilical cord. This vein delivers blood to the baby, mostly through her liver, but also directly down a special blood vessel, the venous duct. Inside the heart is a special fetal circulation involving an opening between the left and right atrium. This reduces the blood flow to the inactive lungs and the flow is further reduced by the presence of an arterial duct that acts as a bypass vessel. In this way, the baby's blood circulation is fine-tuned to its prebreathing condition. After the blood has circulated around the baby's body, waste products and carbon dioxide are returned to the mother via the umbilical arteries.

first breath

Looking at the little newborn from the outside, her proud parents are unaware of the amazing changes taking place inside her tiny body. When the umbilical cord is cut, blocking the oxygen supply from the mother, the resulting sudden rise in carbon dioxide triggers a dramatic reaction that sees the collapsed lungs suddenly expand and take in air. As soon as the baby starts breathing, other changes follow swiftly. The opening in the heart closes and both the arterial and venous ducts shut down. So do the blood vessels that lead from and to the umbilical cord. Now the baby's organs are suddenly sending a greatly increased blood supply to the lungs. In no time at all, the newborn has acquired a miniature version of the adult blood system. And all this is happening internally while the excited parents gaze down at what appears to be a helpless little form in their hands.

a baby's heartbeat

At the moment of birth, a baby's heart beats at an astonishing 180 pulses per minute. Within a few hours this falls to 140 pulses. During the first year of life the rate continues to slow down, but only very gradually. At the age of one year, the infant heart is still beating at 115 pulses per minute, well above the adult resting level of 70–80 pulses per minute. To express it another way, the resting heart rate for an infant is about the same as that for an adult who is performing some kind of strenuous exercise.

digestive system

The stomach of a newborn baby is tiny, but as soon as breathing begins and the baby starts to swallow air, the stomach expands to four or five times its previous size. At the same time, the stomach's position in the baby's abdomen changes. Its capacity at birth is about 1 fluid ounce (30 ml), which doubles within the first week as the milk supply arrives. By the time the baby is about one month old, the size of the stomach has tripled, but is still only one-tenth of the adult condition.

The intestines of a newborn are about 11 feet (3.4 m) in length. This may seem a lot, but the length will have doubled by the time the baby grows to adulthood. The walls of the intestines are unusually thin and the musculature is weak – both features associated with the fact that it is some months before the baby will be able to take solid food. But although the baby's digestive system is poorly developed at birth, it has all the functional capacities needed to cope with liquid food.

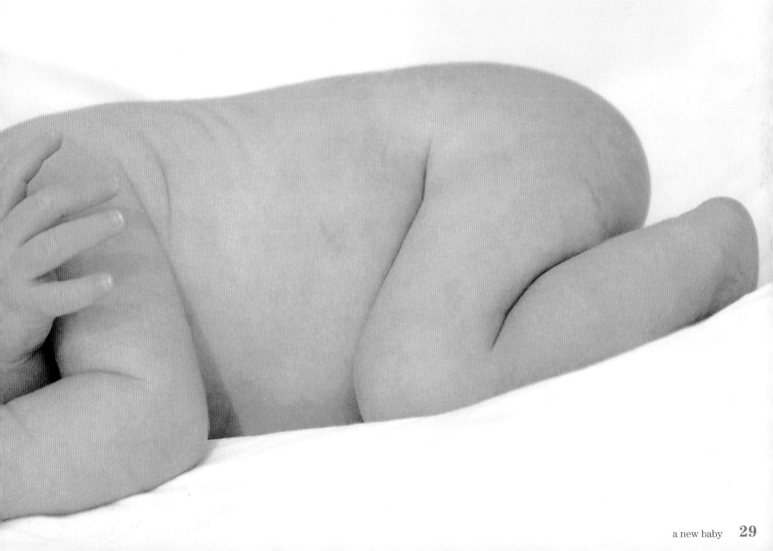

bonding

A newborn baby is programmed to focus his attention on one particular adult – almost always his mother. This protector-figure or "reference person" becomes increasingly important to the baby as he grows and a tight bond starts to develop between the two. Babies who lack this protector may suffer emotionally later in life as a result.

early bonding

For the first few months after birth, human babies are not particularly choosy. They are happy to be cuddled by any caring adult who happens to pick them up. In this respect they are slow starters, because with many animals the newborn becomes tightly bonded with its mother from day one. Usually by about six months (although this may vary from four to eight months) the process begins in earnest for the human infant and he starts to become highly selective in whom he trusts.

A separation anxiety sets in around this time and, from seven to nine months, a baby may scream if a stranger attempts to hold him. At about the same time, a mother begins to be more possessive of her infant and if separated for some reason, the two of them may feel acute distress. The bond has now been formed and will stay with mother and child for years to come.

a special scent

The attachment between a baby and his mother is based on some very ancient abilities. The hormone oxytocin plays a part (see Glands and hormones, page 42), and the sense of smell is also very important. It is not generally known that a baby can identify his own mother by her unique body fragrance, or that a mother can identify her baby in a similar way. Tests have shown, however, that a baby responds positively to the fragrance of his mother's breasts and ignores breast pads used by other women. Even more striking is the discovery that a blindfolded woman has the ability to identify her own child from a host of other babies by scent alone.

the power of voice

A sleeping mother has the ability to identify the particular cry of her own baby. This is another of the bonding factors that has been forgotten because of the way in which we live today. Typically, there is now only one newborn baby in any family house or apartment, so there is no way to test this ability. In an ancient tribe, however, living in small huts in a tiny village settlement, a mother would have been able to hear any of the babies crying in the night. If she woke up every time one of them screamed for food she might get no sleep at all. During the course of evolution she became programmed to awake only at the sound of her own particular infant. This sensitivity is still there to this day, even though it is seldom used.

Similarly, a young baby is also sensitive to his mother's voice. When cradling a baby, most mothers favor the left breast as the resting place for the baby's head. This means that the baby's left ear is more open to the sound of the mother's voice as she intuitively coos to her infant, hums or sings him to sleep. And it is the left ear that feeds information to a baby's right hemisphere – the part of the brain that is especially sensitive to the emotional quality of sounds.

taking root

So, the bond between mother and baby is formed, not just by getting to know each other's faces, but also by becoming fixated on one another's smells and sounds. This emphasizes just how ancient and deep-seated the bonding process is, and how important it is to spend as much time as possible in close company during the early months.

the senses

Your new baby may be entirely dependent on you, but all five senses are ready to receive information about her surroundings so that, eventually, she can fend for herself. Her brain is busy creating important links between nerve cells and so, with each passing month, everything she sees, hears, feels, tastes or smells becomes more meaningful and creates a cell network unique to her alone.

sight

Newborns can see more than was previously thought. Even in the womb a baby is able to distinguish between light and dark. At birth she has good vision up to a distance of 8–10 inches (20–25 cm), which helps her to recognize your face when you hold her in your arms. And she can probably make out an object up to 20 feet (6 m) away. She sees objects best if they are in complete contrast, that is black and white, but she can also distinguish bright, primary colors (although the color cells at the back of her eyes do not develop properly for another couple of months). Her interest in the human face is pronounced – studies show that new babies are more interested in looking at a drawing of a face rather than a random pattern, and they prefer smiling faces to grumpy ones!

Not only are a baby's eyes bigger in relation to her body than those of an adult, her pupils are generally larger too, making her look more appealing and increasing the chances of her being handled more lovingly. Heredity has the biggest influence on eye color, but many green- and brown-eyed children are born with blue eyes since pigment is stimulated by exposure to light and takes about six months to develop.

hearing

Research shows that the inner ear is the only sense organ to develop fully before birth, reaching its adult size by the middle of pregnancy. Within moments of being born, a baby will be startled by loud noises and start to cry. Her hearing is acute and she can recognize your voice and also music or sounds she heard from the womb. She shows more interest in human speech than in other sounds and prefers high-pitched voices.

touch

Your baby's body becomes sensitive to touch soon after conception. By 32 weeks of pregnancy all body parts respond to tactile stimulation. With around 320 touch receptors per square inch (around five million in total), and over 100 different kinds of receptors, a baby responds to pressure, pain, vibrations and changes in temperature. Astonishingly, within a few days of birth she can distinguish between the touch of brush bristles that are of different diameters.

taste

In the womb a fetus swallows amniotic fluid containing traces of her mother's diet. A baby has around 10,000 taste buds (far more than an adult) and these are not just restricted to the tongue but also occur on the mouth sides, back and roof. Eventually these extra taste buds disappear. A baby is able to distinguish between tastes from a very early age, preferring sweet (see Weaning, page 57).

smell

It is hard to know how sensitive a newborn baby is to everyday odors, but studies of two-day-old babies show that they react strongly to certain smells, such as garlic and vinegar. Other studies show that a five-day-old baby turns toward a pad soaked in breast milk, and by 10 days old prefers the smell of her mother's milk to that of another woman. This ability shows how the human baby protects herself from hunger. Even in the dark she is capable of turning toward her source of nourishment. The speed at which a newborn baby learns the fragrance of her own mother is astonishing. Studies show that within 45 hours of birth a baby knows her mother by her smell alone (see Bonding, page 31).

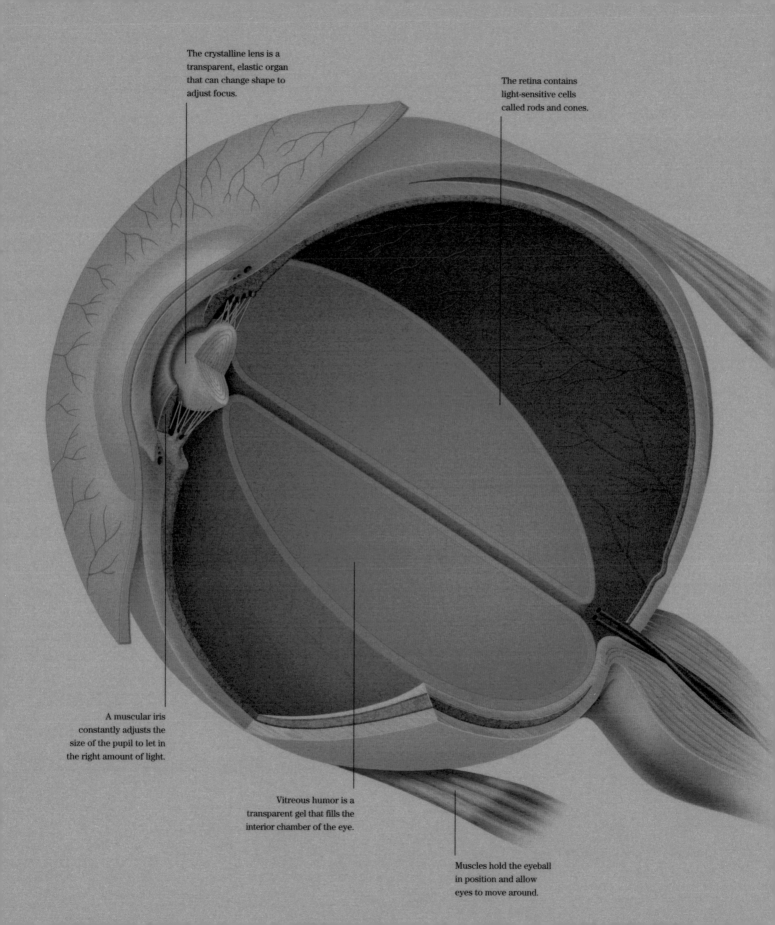

The crystalline lens is a transparent, elastic organ that can change shape to adjust focus.

The retina contains light-sensitive cells called rods and cones.

A muscular iris constantly adjusts the size of the pupil to let in the right amount of light.

Vitreous humor is a transparent gel that fills the interior chamber of the eye.

Muscles hold the eyeball in position and allow eyes to move around.

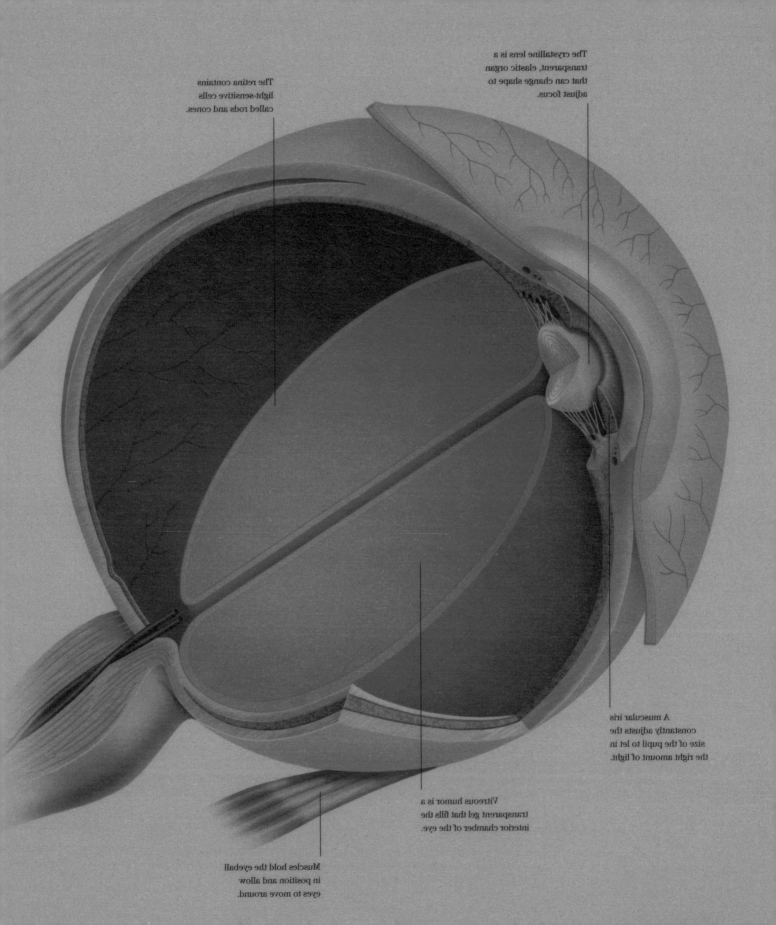

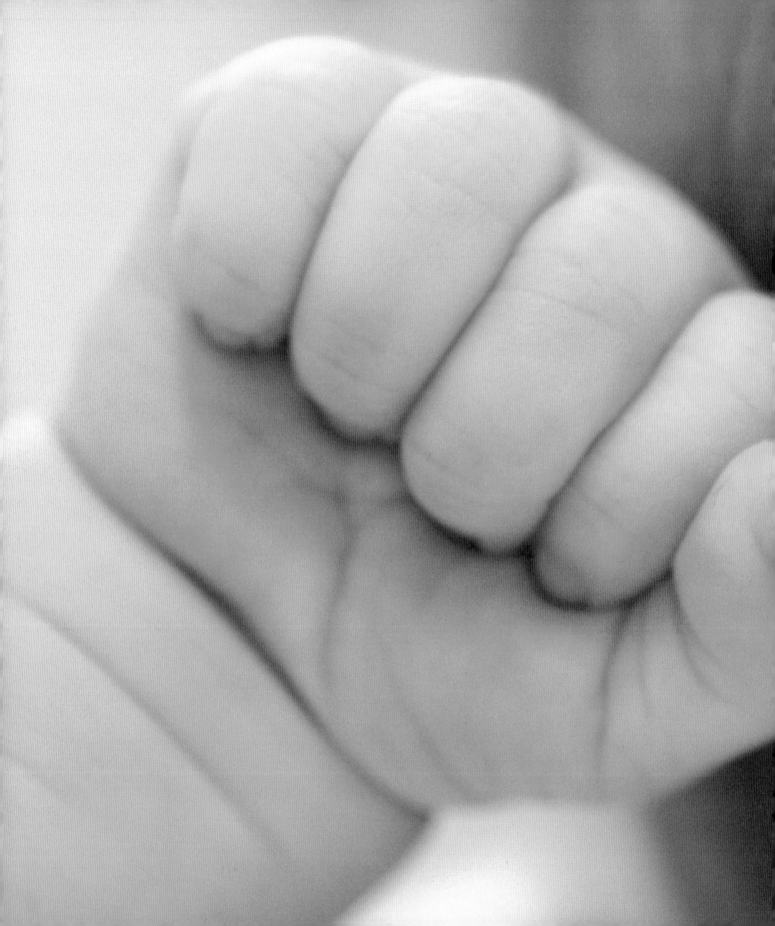

how a baby grows

gestation

Most mammals give birth to a litter of babies, but the human mother typically gestates only one offspring at a time. If her reproductive life continues unhindered, however, she finds herself gestating her second baby while her first is still very young and vulnerable. In this way she may produce a "serial litter" of infants of different ages, all requiring her attention. So, although multiple births may be a rarity for the human mother, she is nevertheless faced with the possibility of caring for a large and very demanding family.

the period of gestation

It is well known that, in human beings, the period between conception and birth lasts for nine months, but this is only a rough guide. Length of gestation varies considerably from woman to woman and a healthy baby may be born anywhere between 240 and 293 days (34 and 42 weeks) after the egg has been fertilized. If born after a pregnancy of fewer than 240 days (34 weeks), a baby is classified as "premature"; if born after more than 293 days (42 weeks) she is said to be "overdue." The most likely length of time between conception and birth is 266 days (38 weeks), or, for those trying to guess the day of the happy event, 280 days (40 weeks) after the last menstrual period (LMP).

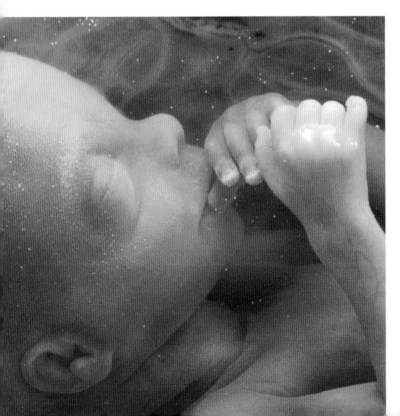

variations

One strange fact about the gestation period is that a female fetus seems to be more reluctant to leave the snug warmth of her mother's womb than her male counterpart. On average, female babies spend a day longer in the womb than male babies. There are also some racial differences. White babies, on average, spend five days longer inside their mothers than black babies, while Indian babies spend six days longer in the womb than white babies. It has been suggested that these geographical differences may have something to do with the size of the babies or the affluence of the mothers, but this is not the case. The variations are purely racial, but nobody knows why they should exist.

optimum conditions

The very best chance a baby has of surviving gestation is when her mother is aged 22. This has been described as "the age of fecundity" in humans, when fetal deaths are at their lowest level – just 12 out of every 1,000. Chances of a trouble-free birth are also extremely good for mothers who are anywhere between the ages of 18 and 30. Older mothers run a slightly increased risk, but even at the age of 45, fetal deaths are still only at the level of 47 in every 1,000. A few women have even managed to give birth in their 50s, although this is extremely rare because the average age for menopause is 51.

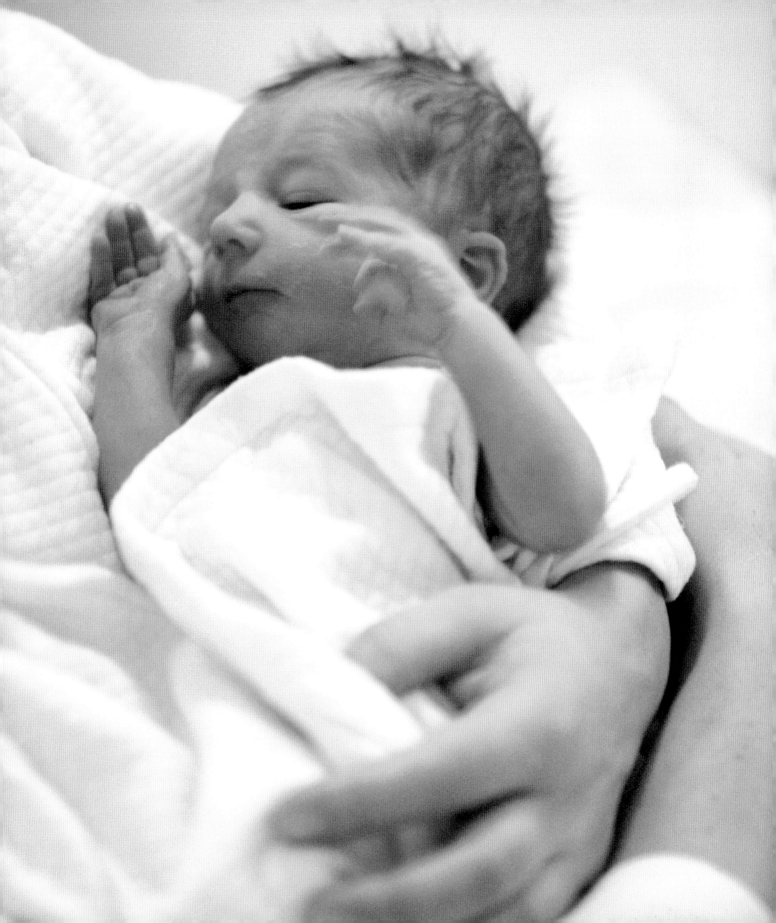

growth in the womb

The baby inside the womb grows at an astonishing rate, but his rapidly changing shape is hidden from us. All we can see is the swelling abdomen of the mother as the time of birth approaches. Thanks to modern technology, however, we do now know a great deal about each phase of the gestational period, from fertilization to birth.

first month

When the egg is fertilized by the sperm it forms a zygote. This divides into a number of cells and eventually becomes hollow, when it is referred to as the blastocyst. This moves down the fallopian tube and becomes attached to the lining of the mother's uterus, a process called implantation. In rare cases, the blastocyst separates into two units, creating what become identical twins. This happens between days five and nine. If it happens later than day nine there is a high risk of conjoined, or Siamese, twins being formed.

Some of the outer cells of the developing embryo become embedded deeply in the lining of the mother's uterus and it is these that eventually become the placenta. Once the dividing cells begin to differentiate, a groove forms that eventually becomes the spinal cord. By the age of three weeks the embryo has grown to a length of ⅛ inch (4 mm) and is already starting to curve into a C-shape. The heart bulge forms and begins to beat, arm buds are present and the embryo now has a tail. At four weeks the embryo has reached ¼ inch (8 mm) in length and the first signs of what will be major organs are beginning to differentiate. Eyes start to develop and nasal pits begin to form. Leg buds are now present and there are paddlelike hands at the ends of the arms.

second month

By the fifth week of growth the embryo measures ½ inch (13 mm) in length and the limbs become more clearly defined – the hands and feet even have digits. The brain is developing and the lungs begin to form. In the sixth week, the length increases to ¾ inch (18 mm) and all major organs have started to develop. Hair follicles, nipples and elbows start to form. Limb movements may already occur. Growth continues fast and in the seventh week the embryo

is 1¼ inches (3 cm) in length and the details of its face and head become more clearly defined, including the eyelids and the external ears. By the eighth week, the embryo has formed all its major organs and from now until birth it is referred to as the fetus. For the next seven months there will be continued growth and organ development, but all the basic structures are by now in place.

third month

The fetus is now 3¼ inches (8 cm) and is, for the first time, able to make a fist by clenching its fingers. Its limbs are longer, the liver is active, the genitals are differentiated and tooth buds begin to show. The fetus closes its eyelids at this stage and does not open them again until the seventh month.

fourth month

During this phase, the fetus doubles its length to 6 inches (15 cm). It performs active movements and its lips make sucking motions. It has hair on its head, the muscles and bones are stronger and the pancreas is active.

fifth month

The fetus is now 8 inches (20 cm) long and its whole body is covered by lanugo (see Newborn skin, page 18). Week 18 sees the appearance of eyelashes, eyebrows, fingernails and toenails. For the first time, the mother senses her baby moving inside her womb, a feeling that is known as the "quickening." It is always an exciting moment because it confirms that there is a real life inside.

sixth month

By the middle of this period the fetus reaches a length of 11 inches (28 cm) and weighs 1 pound 7 ounces (725 g). Footprints and fingerprints are forming on the feet and hands, and the eyes are more fully developed. The lungs contain air sacs. If alarmed by a sudden stimulus, the fetus is capable at this stage of performing the startle reflex (see A baby's reflexes, page 24). Some mothers may not feel the first movements of the baby until the end of this period – the time range for experiencing the quickening varies between 18 and 24 weeks.

seventh month

At around 26 weeks, the fetus reaches 15 inches (38 cm) long and weighs 2½ pounds (1.2 kg). Its eyes are now opening and closing and it can hear noises, such as the sounds of its mother's bodily functions, including her heartbeat, and even sounds like loud music that come from outside the body. The brain, nervous system and respiratory system show rapidly increased development. Babies born prematurely at the end of this month may survive, but the risks are high.

eighth month

By the middle of this period the fetus has probably grown to a length of 17 inches (43 cm), although there is some variation. It weighs about 4 pounds 7 ounces (2 kg). The skeletal structure is fully developed but the bones are not yet hard. There is an increase in the amount of body fat. Babies born during this month are still premature, but the survival rate is slightly better.

ninth month

By the middle of this period the typical fetus is about 19 inches (48 cm) long and weighs up to 6 pounds 9 ounces (3 kg). Its body is getter fatter and it is losing its hairy lanugo coating. The fingernails are nearly full-grown. This is the earliest point at which a birth is not considered to be premature. The shortest gestation that is considered to be full term is 34 weeks (240 days).

10th month

By the middle of this period, the lanugo has gone, and the typical fetus is as much as 21 inches (53 cm) in length. This is the point at which birth is most likely – on the 266th day of gestation, or the 40th week since the last menstrual period (LMP). The amazing journey from fertilized egg to delivered baby is over.

race for life
Each ejaculation contains 400 million sperm. Thousands reach the egg, but usually only one penetrates the outer coat. When the nuclei of sperm and egg fuse, a zygote is formed.

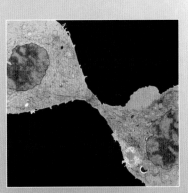

mitotic cell division
The cells of the growing baby multiply by mitosis, a process through which a cell doubles the number of chromosomes in its nucleus and splits into two new, identical daughter cells.

twins

Although the human mother normally only gestates a single baby, in approximately one case out of every 100, two eggs are fertilized at the same time by two different sperm and the mother gives birth to nonidentical twins. In rarer cases – three to four per 1,000 births – one fertilized egg divides into two, creating identical twins. Triplets occur in just one out of every 8,000 births.

conceiving twins

Although rare, the chances of having identical twins seem to stay the same the world over, regardless of genetics or environment. There are, however, certain factors that do increase a woman's chances of having nonidentical twins, for example, if she is older than average when she conceives: by her late 30s her chances rise from 100–1 to 70–1. She is also more likely to conceive nonidentical twins if her body is bigger than average, either taller or fatter, or if she is affluent: at times when food is scarce, say during wartime, the twinning rate drops. Genetics can also play a part and a woman is more likely to have non-identical twins if she is a twin herself or has twin siblings, if she has already had twins or if she has had a number of children already. She may also increase her chances if the sexual act at which conception occurs is unusually passionate (an intensely emotional experience increases the chances of having nonidentical twins) or unusually violent (victims of rape are also more likely to have nonidentical twins).

geographical factors

African women are more likely to have nonidentical twins, whether living in Europe or Africa, making race rather than climate a key factor. The chances of giving birth to twins is especially high in certain parts of West Africa. In Nigeria, for example, it is as high as 22–1. Conversely, women in Japan are less likely to have twins. Here, the odds are as high as 200–1.

a special bond

It is generally accepted that twins do develop closer relationships to one another than different-age siblings. Girl twins in particular are more dependent on each other in infancy and many form a bond that lasts long into adulthood, particularly if they are identical. Boy twins – identical and fraternal – tend to be closer for longer than girl/boy twins.

similar habits

It is not unusual for twins to develop the same or similar habits. Since identical twins have exactly the same DNA, similarities are likely to be evident even if the two children are raised differently or away from one another. Just as they share physical attributes, they may also have similar voices or use the same facial and hand gestures. Fraternal twins, however, share only 50 percent of their DNA, the same as regular siblings. Another reason for the close bond and similar behavior of twins may result from the babies having spent their time in the womb together, as well as the first few weeks bonding with mother.

cryptic messages

A number of twins appear to develop a secret language that only they can understand. Known as cryptophasia, this often happens in late-developers and it is thought that the more advanced twin in terms of speech establishes a form of baby talk that the sibling can both understand and mimic. It may also be the case that cryptophasia occurs in infants who have less adult interaction than perhaps they would have done if they were single children.

glands and hormones

The activities of a baby's body are controlled by two major systems: the nervous system and the endocrine system. The endocrine glands produce special chemicals that are released into the bloodstream, circulate through the body and reach receptors in the cells, via which they influence cellular metabolism. These chemicals, the hormones, exert major influences on the body's growth and development and control the baby's internal environment.

pituitary gland

Despite its important role in controlling growth, this tiny gland is only 1/8 inch (4 mm) across at birth. It sits snugly like a little pellet at the base of the brain, just below the hypothalamus. The hypothalamus itself is the link between the nervous system and the endocrine system. One of its tasks is to produce neurohormones that control the activities of the pituitary.

The pituitary gland is formed in the embryo by the end of the second month of pregnancy and very soon starts work. It has two main roles: sending growth hormones to the body's cells and sending special hormones to the thyroid gland that trigger it into action. The impact of the pituitary gland, as the infant develops, is to stimulate cell division and DNA formation.

thyroid gland

Taking its instructions from the pituitary, the thyroid gland produces thyroxine, a hormone that also promotes growth and development, especially of the bones, teeth and brain, and helps to regulate the general metabolism of the body. Its shape has been described as resembling a butterfly or a bow tie, as it has two side lobes joined by a narrow isthmus. It is positioned in the neck region, just below the larynx.

pancreas

The pancreas, situated in the baby's abdomen, weighs 1/8–1/4 ounces (3–5 g) at birth, just one-thirtieth of its adult weight. By the end of the first year this increases to 1/2 ounce (10 g). The function of the pancreas is to secrete an alkaline juice to aid in the digestion of food, as well as the two opposing hormones, glucagon and insulin, to maintain a balance in the blood glucose level.

the bonding hormone

The endocrine system is extremely complex and involves many different kinds of hormones, each with its particular influence on the baby's body, but there is one that deserves a special mention. This is the hormone called oxytocin, sometimes referred to as the "bonding hormone" or, more romantically, the "hormone of love." It is made in the hypothalamus and released into the blood system via the posterior lobe of the pituitary gland.

When we speak of the "chemistry" between two young lovers, oxytocin is the chemical in question. When couples who describe themselves as "madly in love" are tested, they are found to have higher than normal levels of oxytocin. During orgasm there is a sudden burst of oxytocin, revealing that these peak moments of sexual pleasure also function as powerful bonding experiences. Making love literally makes love. And a similar process occurs between a mother and her baby.

As a woman gives birth, her endocrine system releases oxytocin, preparing her chemically to feel loving toward the tiny being she is about to hold in her arms. Some of the oxytocin crosses the placenta and also helps to reduce the stress levels of the baby after the painful pressures of birth. Later, breast-feeding causes a further release of oxytocin, creating relaxation and feelings of emotional attachment.

loving touch

Interestingly, with bottle-fed babies there is a hormonal difference between those who are fed rather mechanically, and those who are given the bottle while at the same time being closely cuddled by the parent. The cuddled infants show higher levels of oxytocin, revealing that the hormone's release in the baby can be stimulated simply by loving contact.

It follows from this that, during the early days of infancy, the more intimate contact there is, the stronger will be the emotional attachment, thanks to the high levels of oxytocin that are being maintained. Furthermore, the baby that experiences prolonged elevated levels of this hormone during the earliest days will also enjoy a great reduction in stress-hormone responses. This can have a lasting effect, helping to create a secure adult later in life.

the master gland
At least nine different hormones are released by the pituitary gland located in the head. These include important growth hormones that stimulate cell division and DNA formation for the baby's developing brain, bones and muscles.

a baby's appearance

One of the great joys for parents is watching their baby change, day by day, month by month and year by year. As the baby's hair and skin color are modified, the limbs become longer in relation to the body and the silhouette becomes more streamlined, parents start to detect family likenesses and witness the fascinating ways in which their plump, helpless baby develops into a stronger, increasingly active toddler.

In the first three months, the skin loses its redness and may begin to darken. By four months the eyes will have reached their final color and are likely to have lost any squint. The hair that the baby was born with may fall out in the early weeks, to be replaced with hair of a slightly coarser texture. Some babies, on the other hand, are still bald at one year, and hair may not reach its final color for several years. As the bones harden, the baby's once rubbery, flexible body becomes gradually stiffer and more able to pull itself erect, first sitting, then crawling and then, eventually, standing (see pages 74–79).

These pictures show one particular growing infant, from just after birth to the age of one year. The newborn baby has short limbs bent up in a prenatal position. There is plenty of room for him to stretch out his arms and legs, but the cramped space inside the womb has left a curled-up legacy that will take some time to disappear. As he grows, his top half develops slighter faster and his arms straighten out first. Even up to nine months, it is clear that the legs still favor a bent-up position, while the hands are reaching out more and more. Then, at one year, the legs have caught up with the arms and now the infant can, at last, stand tall.

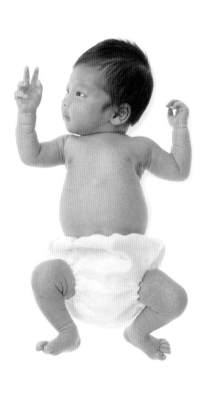

appeal of the baby face

The German word *kinderschema* is used to explain the special appeal of the baby face. Human adults are genetically programmed to respond protectively and lovingly toward a face with a particular set of features and it is no accident that these features are found in their most exaggerated form on the face of a baby. The *kinderschema* is made up of the following elements: a big head in relation to the body, a flat face, a large domed forehead, a small button nose, big low-lying eyes, fat rounded cheeks, soft, warm skin, very fine hair and a small, receding chin.

Research has located the reaction to the *kinderschema* in the medial orbitofrontal cortex, a part of the brain associated with emotional responses. Tests found that, when an adult was presented with the face of an unfamiliar baby, this part of the brain reacted within one-seventh of a second, a speed that indicates that the response must be instinctual. So powerful is the human response to this configuration of facial features that pet animals that have similar qualities will also arouse strong parental feelings and selective breeding has flattened the faces of some cats and dogs, giving them a greater appeal to "pseudo parents."

In humans, the baby face elements are retained for a long time and the fully angular adult facial proportions do not appear until puberty. But, as the years of childhood pass, the *kinderschema* signals become slightly weaker. They are at their strongest during the first two years of life, when the infant is at his most helpless. In addition to the face, the baby's short, stubby limbs, rounded contours, soft flexibility of body and general clumsiness of movement also transmit special signals to the adult, saying "look after me" and triggering a protective reaction.

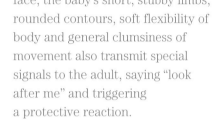

a baby's growth

At birth, the typical weight for a baby is 7½ pounds (3.5 kg). By 12 months, this has roughly trebled and, by the end of the first two years of life outside the womb, it has multiplied by four. By this time, at two years old, an infant is approximately half her adult height.

your unique baby

There is great variation, however, not only in body weight, but also in height and growth rate. If a particular baby is slightly smaller or larger there is no need for concern providing she is showing a gradual increase. To give some idea of the huge variations that exist, the average weight of a baby at birth is 7–8 pounds (3–4 kg), but the heaviest baby ever born weighed over 22 pounds (10 kg) – seven times the average. The smallest baby ever to survive (a premature one) weighed only 8½ ounces (265 g) at birth. These are extreme examples, of course, but they do give some idea of the amazing range of sizes at which babies can enter the world and survive. Despite this, an idea of average figures for a typical baby is useful to have, even if it only serves as a rough guide.

boys and girls

The size and weight of a baby may depend on a number of circumstances, as will the rate of growth. One significant factor is the baby's sex. On the whole baby boys are larger and heavier than baby girls. For example, the average weight of a newborn boy is 7 pounds 10 ounces (3.6 kg), while that of a newborn girl is 7 pounds 2 ounces (3.2 kg). By the end of his first year, an average baby boy weighs 22 pounds 13 ounces (10.3 kg), while an average girl weighs 21 pounds 2 ounces (9.5 kg). And at the age of two years, their average weights are 28 pounds 4 ounces (12.7 kg) and 26 pounds 10 ounces (12.1 kg) respectively.

other factors

The timing of a baby's birth might also influence growth. Premature babies tend to be smaller and lighter than average, as do multiples – twins and triplets – often because they are also premature: the average length of a twin pregnancy is 36 weeks. Other significant factors include genetics – babies of tall parents tend to be tall themselves, for example; nutrition – bottle-fed babies gain weight more rapidly than breast-fed babies; and ethnic origin – average birth height varies in different regions of the world.

diet after weaning

The successful continued growth of the infant is dependent on her receiving a balanced diet. As a baby belongs to a species that evolved as omnivores, she ideally needs foods of both animal and plant origin after she has been weaned. Some people believe that it is wrong to give an infant any foods derived from animals, but this puts the growing child at a disadvantage. Per unit body weight, the protein requirements for infants are four times as high as those for adults. Only a diet that includes animal proteins can supply the human digestive system with the ideal amino-acid balance. Interestingly, we all ingest some animal proteins in the form of grubs and insects consumed inadvertently as they find their way into foodstuffs such as cereals and grains, vegetables and fruit.

the skeleton

We usually think of bones as inert but inside the body they are very much alive, and as a baby grows his bones undergo dramatic change. The bones of a baby are much softer, more spongy, more porous and have a higher water content than those of an adult. During the first two years of life they grow in size (an adult skeleton weighs 25 times that of a baby), harden and many fuse together. The flexible skeleton that suited the cramped space inside the uterus develops into the strong, stiff scaffolding that supports an increasingly active body.

the hardening process

In the womb, the skeleton of a fetus forms not from bone, but from a softer, more pliable material called cartilage that allows easier growth. As the fetus increases in size, a process of ossification begins in which parts of the developing skeleton become harder and eventually transform into bone. After birth, the calcium a baby obtains from his mother's milk is crucial in aiding this process.

At birth, parts of the skeleton are still in the cartilaginous condition, which is why a newborn is so floppy and helpless. The process of hardening is completed as the child grows to adulthood. It is only as the cartilage hardens to bone that the child is gradually able to control his movements – from sitting, to standing, to crawling, to walking, to running and jumping.

how many bones?

A skeleton has two major parts. The first is the central or axial skeleton, consisting of the skull, the small bones of the middle ear, the hyoid bone in the throat, the vertebral column and the chest bones. The second part is the limb or appendicular skeleton, comprising the shoulder girdle, the arms and hands, the pelvic girdle and the legs and feet. An adult human being has a skeleton made up of 206 bones, far fewer than are found in the skeleton of a newborn. The exact number of infant bones varies from baby to baby, but there are usually about 270 at birth.

Reductions in the number of bones take place in the central skeleton, owing to the fusing together of separate bones in the skull and in the spine. There are 172 bones in this part of the skeleton at birth, but only 80 in the adult. At the same time, increases in the number of bones take place in the limb skeleton, owing to more bones developing in the wrists and ankles. There are only 98 bones in this part of the skeleton at birth, but 126 in the adult. So, together, there are 92 losses and 28 gains, a difference of 64, which accounts for the drop from 270 birth bones to 206 adult bones.

bones that fuse together

As a baby grows, many of the 45 bony elements of the newborn skull fuse together until, as an adult, he has only 22 skull bones – eight forming the braincase and 14 supporting the face. At the base of the spine there are five separate bones at birth. These sacral bones become fused together as a single bony structure in the adult.

new bones

The long bones in the body, found in the arms and legs, must undergo a massive growth spurt once the baby has been released from the confines of the womb. There are special parts of these bones, called growth plates, where the cartilage cells divide and increase in number. The older cartilage cells move gradually toward the middle of the bone where they are eventually replaced by hard bone. Only when the whole bone has been ossified do the growth plates themselves harden and become converted into bone.

The limb extremities undergo a major change during infancy. At birth there are no ossified carpal (wrist) bones and only two tarsal (ankle) bones. Even at one year, an infant only has three wrist bones compared with the eight he eventually has when he becomes an adult. A baby is also born without ossified kneecaps. These do not develop until he is about two years old, and frequently much older.

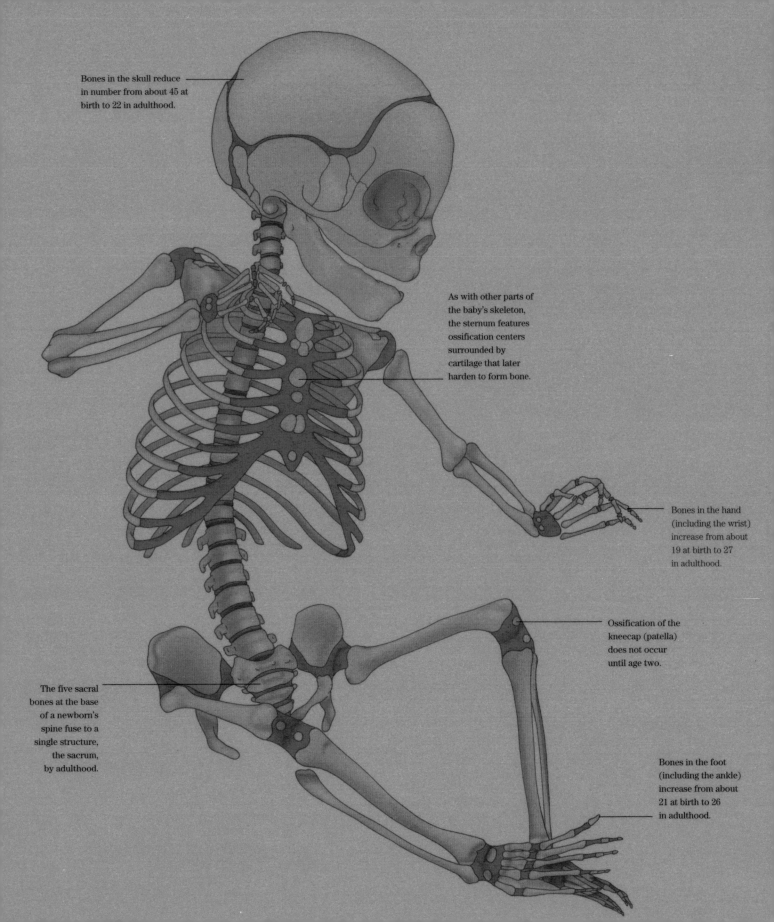

Bones in the skull reduce in number from about 45 at birth to 22 in adulthood.

As with other parts of the baby's skeleton, the sternum features ossification centers surrounded by cartilage that later harden to form bone.

Bones in the hand (including the wrist) increase from about 19 at birth to 27 in adulthood.

Ossification of the kneecap (patella) does not occur until age two.

The five sacral bones at the base of a newborn's spine fuse to a single structure, the sacrum, by adulthood.

Bones in the foot (including the ankle) increase from about 21 at birth to 26 in adulthood.

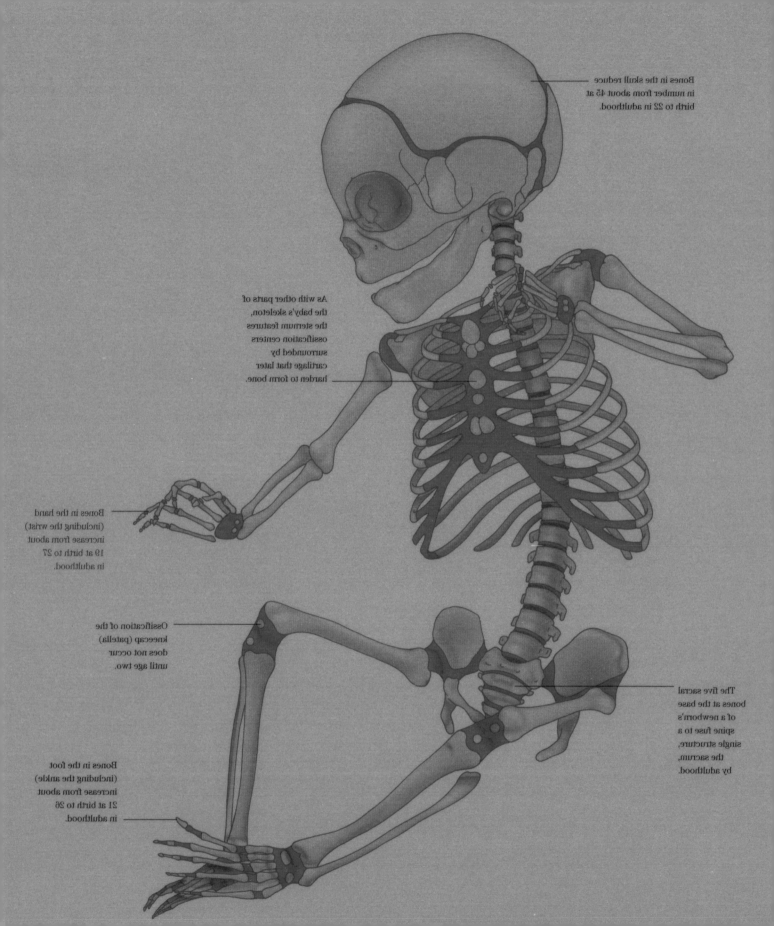

growth of the bones

This X-ray of a toddler's hand shows areas of cartilage in the joints between the finger bones, where bone formation and growth will take place. As yet, only a few of the wrist bones have formed.

the nervous system

While there are visible signs of physical growth that a parent can watch and measure, there are also important invisible changes taking place inside a growing infant. The most important of these is the slow growth of the nervous system. At each age, a baby's ability is determined by what stage of development her nervous system has reached – a process that cannot be rushed without causing the baby distress.

The nervous system develops at its own set pace, with more and more refined controls coming into play as the weeks pass. To expect a baby to show a control that her nervous system has not yet mastered is asking the impossible. Equally, to deny a baby the opportunity to express the developmental stage she has reached holds her back and frustrates her.

brain size

At birth, a baby's brain is well developed in relation to the rest of her body. In particular it is much larger in relation to the rest of the head than it is in adulthood, giving the infant a slightly top-heavy look. The brain of a newborn accounts for 10 percent of her total body weight. In adults, this figure is down to 2 percent. The birth weight of the brain is about 11½ ounces (350 g), with a cranial capacity of 400 cc, compared with a weight of 2–3½ pounds (1.1–1.7 kg) in the adult and a cranial capacity of 1,300 to 1,500 cc. By the end of her first year of life, an infant's brain increases in size by about two and a half times, and by the end of the fifth year it is three times what it was at birth. At all stages the male brain is slightly larger than that of the female.

brain function

The newborn brain has a lot to learn! Those regions concerned with sleeping and waking, with feeding and excreting – essentially the hindbrain and the midbrain – are already active, but those parts that deal with such matters as controlled movement, complex thinking and language – the cerebral cortex – take several years to develop fully. At birth, the cortex is the least developed part of the brain. Refinements appear slowly, showing subtle improvements and increasingly delicate adjustments every week of a baby's early life (see The brain, page 128).

growth of the neural network

One of the challenges facing a newborn brain is the need to send messages to the various parts of the body via the nervous system – a system that is far from ready for this important task, particularly at the body's extremities. This is because a nerve sheath called "myelin" must develop to encase the nerves before they can transmit their signals efficiently. The myelin insulates the nerve fibers from one another, making it easier for them to transmit nervous impulses. The growth of the major part of these protective sheaths takes about two years to complete and it occurs in stages, with the head end of the body developing first, then the trunk. The parts of the limbs nearest to the trunk develop fine control before the extremities, with fine control of the digits coming later. The development of myelin sheaths in the brain itself takes much longer and continues right up to adolescence.

feeding the brain

As the neural network grows and develops, there is a set sequence in which an infant advances from her helpless, newborn condition to her much more controlled active state as a two-year-old. First come improved coordination and balance, followed by increasing skill with voluntary movements. Improvements in hearing, vision and understanding words and the beginnings of speech come next, then refinements in attention, memory, creativity, planning and monitoring behavior. During this long process, the more the infant's brain is stimulated by its environment, the better its growth. It needs a rich input to file away in its "biological computer" so that, later on, it has an "experience bank" to draw upon. An infant in a bleak, unvarying environment will clearly be at a disadvantage and this is true even at the earliest stages of development.

feeding

Before a baby is weaned on to solid foods, he survives entirely on milk supplied by his mother's breasts or from a bottle. This applies for the first six months, after which a baby can eat a little solid food as well. From this time, the proportion of solid food can slowly increase while breast- or bottle-feeding continues. Between about the ninth and 12th months a baby moves on to the next major phase of feeding himself (see Weaning, page 57).

sucking

A baby is said to suck milk from a nipple, but the action is more like squeezing than sucking. The infant's lips take hold of the pigmented skin around the nipple and he squeezes on this with his jaws and tongue. The pressure he creates in this way forces the milk through the nipple and into his mouth. The nipple itself is not sucked on, therefore, but acts as a nozzle for milk delivery. During the first year, a blister known as a sucking pad may form on the baby's lip as a result of his sucking action.

Once a newborn baby starts feeding at the breast he usually closes his eyes and concentrates on the pleasures of tasting and swallowing the milk. Later, when he is a few months old, this changes and he starts to keep his eyes open more and more while he swallows the milk. It is during this phase that prolonged eye contact between mother and infant play an important role in strengthening the bond of attachment between them.

premilk

The first liquid a newborn baby obtains from the breast is a kind of premilk called "colostrum." This is a yellowish liquid, rich in proteins and antibodies that help to protect the newborn baby from infections. The mother's breasts continue to supply this important first food for about three days, after which true milk begins to flow. True milk is twice as rich in fat and sugar as colostrum and is so nutritious that the infant soon begins to gain weight rapidly.

the feeding session

Once true milk is delivered, a special sequence develops during each breast-feeding session. At first the breast produces foremilk and then, later in the feed, hind milk.

The foremilk is thin, watery and serves primarily as a thirst quencher. The hind milk is thicker and much richer, satisfying the baby's need for nourishment. It is as if the breast is saying to the baby "drink first, then feed." This highlights one of the disadvantages of very short sessions at the breast; they may help a thirsty baby, but they do not provide him with a satisfying intake of food. To complete the full feeding cycle, a baby needs to spend between 10 and 15 minutes on one breast.

feeding on demand

The current practice of "demand feeding" has been used by tribal mothers since prehistoric times. It operates on the simple premise that a baby feeds whenever he is hungry. There may be a higher number of feeding sessions using this method, but there are also advantages: the more frequent feeds prevent the breasts from becoming engorged and the baby is less likely to overfeed at each session. Moreover, the baby feeds at a natural rate: he develops his own routine and becomes "self-scheduling," automatically reducing the number of feeds he demands as time goes by.

advantages of breast milk

For mothers who are unable to breast-feed, bottle-feeding provides a viable alternative. However, breast milk has evolved over a million years to give the baby exactly what he needs. Not only does breast milk provide antibodies in the earliest days of infancy, but it is also well balanced, nutritionally. The close body contact required for breast-feeding and the flesh-to-flesh intimacy involved serve to strengthen the bond of attachment between mother and child. This is not entirely lost with bottle-feeding, but is inevitably less intense.

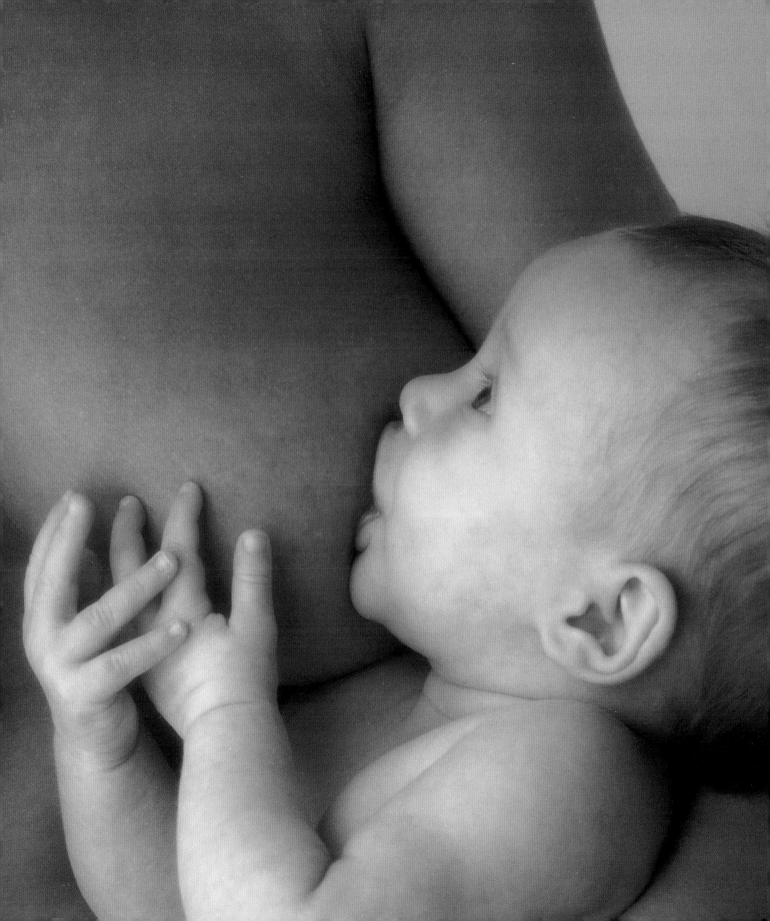

tooth development

A baby's teeth start to develop while she is still inside the womb, but the first one to emerge from the gums usually appears when she is about six months old. It is normally one of the central lower incisors, or cutting teeth, and is soon followed by the other central incisors, both lower and upper.

Next come the lateral incisors, appearing between seven and 11 months. Then there are the first molars, or chewing teeth, at between 10 and 16 months, followed by the canines, or pointed teeth, at 16 to 20 months. Finally come the second molars, to give the full complement of baby teeth by about the age of two years. These baby teeth stay in use until the child has reached the age of six or seven, when they start to be displaced by the adult, permanent teeth that erupt just behind them. There are 20 baby teeth in total, compared with 32 adult teeth: eight incisors, four canines and eight molars. Adults have the same number of incisors and canines, but also have eight premolars and 12 molars.

the body's hardest substance

The tooth is the only part of the human body that cannot repair itself when damaged or broken and, despite the fact that tooth enamel is the hardest substance in the body, it is prone to attack from acids and sugars in the food that we eat. Saliva production goes some way to reducing the effects of harmful substances. Produced constantly throughout the day, more so at times of feeding, saliva helps to keep the mouth clean and free of debris. It also has antibacterial, antiviral and antifungal properties.

teething problems

While some babies develop all of their teeth with seemingly little discomfort, others suffer terribly from the pain. Although a baby cannot tell her parents what is troubling her, a number of telltale signs indicate that she is cutting a new tooth. She looks flushed and has an increased temperature. Inside her mouth her gums are red and swollen and she drools and dribbles with the excess saliva that is produced during teething. Many babies grab and chew anything that comes within reach in an attempt to alleviate the pain. Emotionally, teething babies become quite distraught, whining repeatedly with the pain and generally becoming more clingy.

babies born with teeth

At birth, one in 2,000 babies displays what is called a "natal tooth" – a single tooth that gleams from the newborn's mouth. When present, these natal teeth interfere with the sucking action during either breast-feeding or bottle-feeding, and they are usually removed both for the comfort of the mother and the safety of the baby. If they are left in place they can easily damage the newborn's tongue during feeding sessions.

weaning

Today, mothers are advised to breast- or bottle-feed their babies exclusively for the first six months, after which they should begin to introduce solid foods gradually, while still breast- or bottle-feeding. Between six and nine months, the proportion of smooth and textured solid foods slowly increases until, by the end of the first year of life, most babies are happily feeding themselves.

primitive weaning

How did human mothers wean their babies before the advent of specially designed baby food? How did prehistoric women manage to make this important transition? The answer is that they did what many other animals do – they fed their babies mouth-to-mouth with premasticated food. The mother herself chewed food until it was a soft mass, almost like a warm soup. She then pressed her lips against those of her infant and pushed her tongue into his mouth. The baby reacted to the presence of the tongue as if it were the nipple and started sucking. In this way he ingested the masticated food and the weaning process began.

modern weaning

Today, weaning is simple. Mechanical blenders and jars of commercial baby foods are available almost everywhere. But despite the ease with which one can offer weaning food to babies, it is crucially important not to rush the process. Solid food should be introduced very slowly, little by little, as the breast milk or bottled milk is equally slowly reduced in quantity. A sudden, major switch from milk to solids is not advisable: at least three months should be allowed for the complete diet change.

taste preferences

Surprisingly, a baby has more taste buds than an adult and they are more widely distributed inside the mouth. In addition to taste buds on the tongue, he also has them on the palate, the back of the throat, the tonsils and even on the insides of his cheeks. There are four basic tastes: bitter, salt, sour and sweet. If a baby is offered each of these tastes singly, in turn, he hates the first three and loves the fourth. In his early months, he likes only sweet things. All other tastes produce grimaces, attempts at rejection and, if all else fails, angry crying.

from liquids to solids

The progress of the infant from liquids to soft food to solids may require some patience on the part of parents. A baby, favoring only the sweetest tastes, does not always take kindly to a more varied diet. Some authorities suggest that the "sweet tooth" must be defeated early on in the weaning process. The fear is that if babies are weaned solely on very sweet, soft foods – such as banana purée – they become so addicted to sweetness that it is difficult to encourage them to eat enough nonsweet foods when they reach the stage where their health requires a much more varied diet.

sleep and dreams

As new parents soon discover, their baby's sleeping pattern is very different from their own. A newborn baby sleeps twice as long as an adult, but in short bursts rather than for long periods. And to begin with she sleeps as much during the day as at night. It is impossible to modify this infantile sleeping pattern and, for the first weeks of parenthood at least, it is the adults who must adapt.

sleeping time

During her first week of life outside the womb, a typical baby sleeps for a total of 16.6 hours out of every 24. This total sleep time may be split up into as many as 18 separate naps. It is not unusual, however, for an infant to sleep for much more or much less than this, as there is considerable individual variation. Indeed, some babies snooze for a total of only 10.5 hours out of every 24, while others are very sleepy indeed, slumbering for a total of 23 out of every 24.

By the time a baby is four weeks old, her total sleep time is about two hours shorter. The average month-old baby sleeps for 14¾ hours and this reduces further to just under 14 hours at the age of six months. At one year, the figure drops to an average of 13 hours and it continues to shorten throughout childhood. By the age of five years it is down to 12 hours out of every 24, and then slowly decreases to the adult level of about eight hours.

This gradual reduction in sleep time is more marked during the hours of daylight. This is evident as early as the third week, when there is already a slight difference in daytime and nighttime sleeping. The three-week-old baby sleeps for just 54 percent of the daylight hours, but still slumbers for 72 percent of the night hours. By the time she has reached her 26th week, these figures change to 28 percent and 83 percent respectively. Daylight is now a time for short naps and parents can relax a little more at night, as the baby often enjoys 10 hours of uninterrupted sleep. Soon there is only one morning nap and one afternoon siesta, and then, by the time the baby celebrates her first birthday, the morning nap finally vanishes.

types of sleep

There are two, very different kinds of slumber. The first is dreaming sleep and the second is deep sleep. During dreaming sleep the eyelids flicker and, beneath them, the eyes move rapidly this way and that. For this reason, dreaming sleep is known technically as rapid eye movement (REM) sleep. Adults spend about a third of their total sleeping time in this REM phase, but with babies it accounts for as much as a half or even two-thirds.

During the REM phase, the blood supply to the brain is greatly increased and this can benefit a baby's learning ability. When she is awake, she is more alert, her ability to process and retain information is increased and her senses are heightened. During the phases of deep, dreamless sleep, a baby's body restores itself, with blood directed to the developing muscles, the release of growth hormones and the more rapid division of tissue cells.

the dreaming baby

Of course, it is impossible to know what a baby dreams about, but there must be a huge amount of information for her to digest every 24 hours. A newborn baby enters the REM phase as soon as she falls asleep, unlike an older baby who first sinks into the deep, dreamless phase of sleep. If you watch a sleeping baby it is easy to see which phase she is in. Apart from her rapid eye movements when dreaming, she also twitches occasionally and her breathing may become slightly irregular. When she stops dreaming and sinks into the deeper sleep, the baby's body becomes motionless with her muscles relaxed and a peaceful expression on her face.

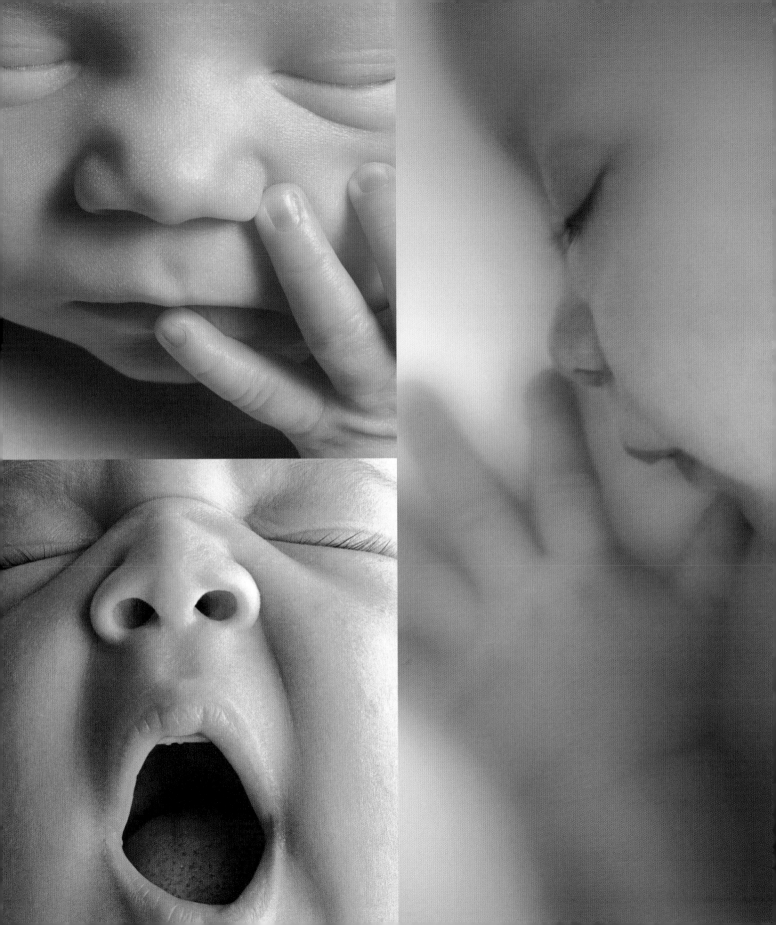

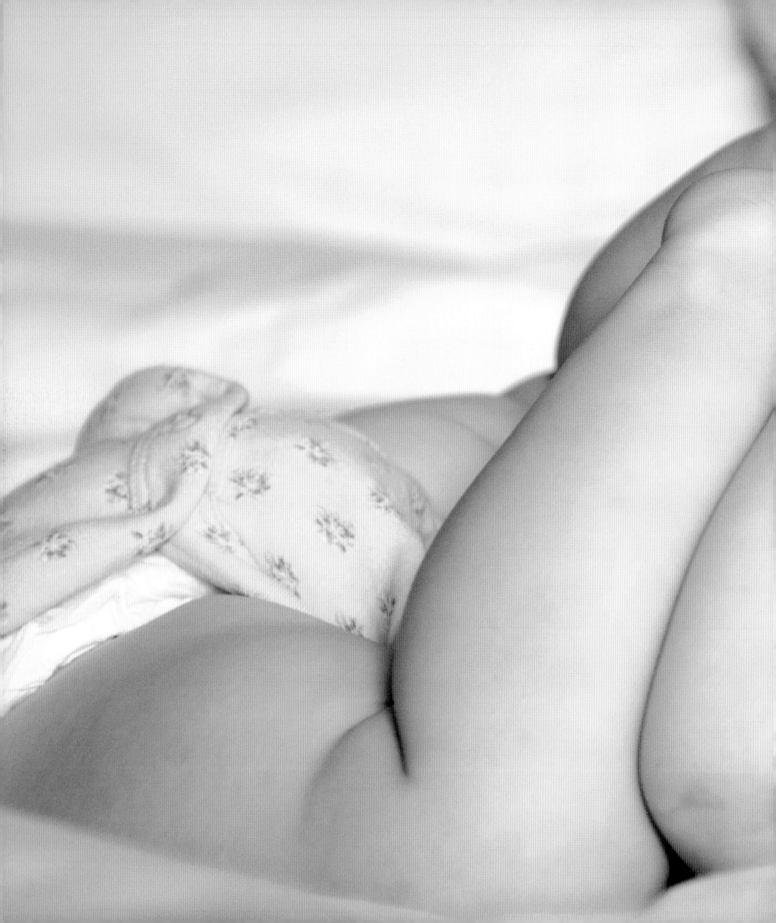

on the move

becoming mobile

Some young animals run around from the day they are born, but the human baby must wait several months before she can perform any kind of locomotion. Her body movements develop gradually and very slowly, in a predictable sequence.

first movements

The very first movements a baby makes are little more than gentle actions when exploring her mother's breast at feeding time. From these first clumsy touches she soon develops a variety of simple squeezing, grasping and rubbing motions as she investigates the surfaces around her. She soon learns to tell the difference between hard and soft, rough and smooth, cool and warm.

Although a baby may kick and wave her arms around if she attempts to move her whole body at this very early stage, her actions usually go no further than squirming or wriggling when she is uncomfortable or miserable. Her first real body movement comes when she discovers that, if she digs her heels in and kicks, she is thrust forward. Despite this small triumph, the first few weeks of a baby's life are truly helpless.

from chin-up to chest-up to bottom-up

Mobility slowly increases as the weeks pass. Placed on her front, a baby strains to lift her chin off the ground, as though she is not happy with this particular position. This first happens at about four weeks, although proper head control does not arrive for several months yet and her heavy head continues to need support when held. In her attempts to raise herself up, the head end of the baby is always slightly more advanced than the rear end.

At the age of about 16 weeks, a baby is capable of pushing upward with her arms and, a little later, manages to do the same with her legs. At first, however, she can only achieve these chest-up and bottom-up postures one at a time. It is as if she is preparing to crawl on her hands and feet by perfecting the two halves of the action separately, but she still cannot do both simultaneously. Perhaps in frustration, she may start to rotate on to her side at this point, finding that she can move herself around by rolling along.

from slither to crawl to walk

The next phase sees the development of the "slither" – a sort of commando crawl – in which a baby drags herself forward with her tummy on the ground, and uses both arms and legs to propel herself along. At seven months she at last finds that she can sit up unaided and control her sitting posture. Her body is stronger now and, at about eight months, the full crawl begins and the baby is, for the first time, truly mobile. This phase persists for several months until the baby struggles to adopt the vertical posture, first with parental help and then on her own. Once she can stand, walking is imminent and the baby becomes a toddler.

the muscles

Born with little muscular ability, the newborn baby has a greater degree of muscle control by 24 weeks of age. A parent can help by supporting the baby while he is sitting or standing, and watching as he makes an effort to maintain the position. He may not succeed but, in the process of trying, a baby learns something about his developing muscle systems by testing out the upper limits of his various body postures and movements.

muscle growth

A baby possesses all of his muscle fibers when he is born, although at this stage they are small and watery. As they grow, these neonatal fibers become longer, thicker and less watery. This development progresses in a "head to tail" sequence, with the muscles nearer the head end of the body always being slightly in advance of those to the rear. When a baby finally reaches adulthood, his muscles are 40 times as strong as they were at birth. Male babies have more muscle tissue than female babies, a difference that persists throughout life, and their physical growth is more variable than that of female babies.

types of muscle

Like an adult, a baby has three kinds of muscle. Striped, or striated, muscles are the voluntary muscles that operate the movements of the limbs, neck and face. They are all attached to the skeleton and are sometimes referred to as "skeletal muscles." As a baby grows, he develops more and more precise control over the actions of these muscles.

Smooth muscles are involuntary. There is no conscious control over them and their activities go unnoticed unless something is wrong. Smooth muscles control the movement of food through the intestines, the circular ones squeezing the gut and the longitudinal ones widening it. Smooth muscles also control the salivary glands, squeezing them during eating and moistening the food. The iris of the eye, changing with the intensity of the light, is also operated automatically by smooth muscles.

Cardiac muscles are striped, but are also involuntary. They automatically create a steady heartbeat, and one that can speed up or slow down according to the amount of physical activity taking place. They also speed up the heartbeat during moments of fear, anger or anxiety because these are moods that anticipate increased physical activity (which may or may not ultimately occur).

working in pairs

All three muscle types can contract themselves actively but can only expand passively. They must therefore work in opposing pairs, one of them forcibly contracting while its opposite number relaxes and allows itself to be stretched out. For example, if the biceps muscles in the arm contract, the arm bends. Then, if the triceps muscles contract, the arm straightens itself again. As the arm moves back and forth, there is no active muscle stretching, but simply two opposing contractions. The power of this system is weak in the newborn baby but slowly gathers strength as he grows.

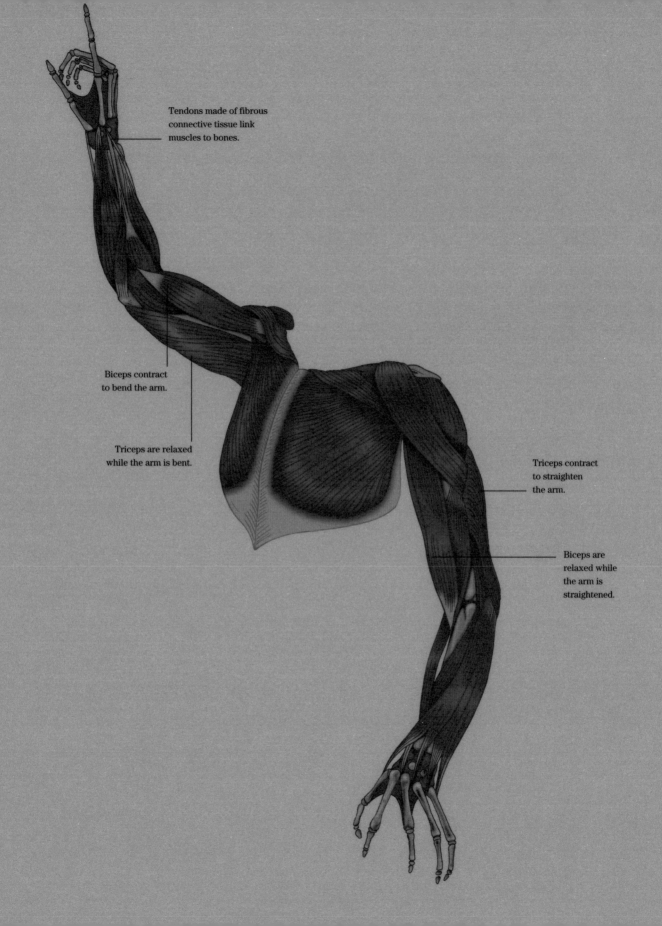

Tendons made of fibrous
connective tissue link
muscles to bones.

Biceps contract
to bend the arm.

Triceps are relaxed
while the arm is bent.

Triceps contract
to straighten
the arm.

Biceps are
relaxed while
the arm is
straightened.

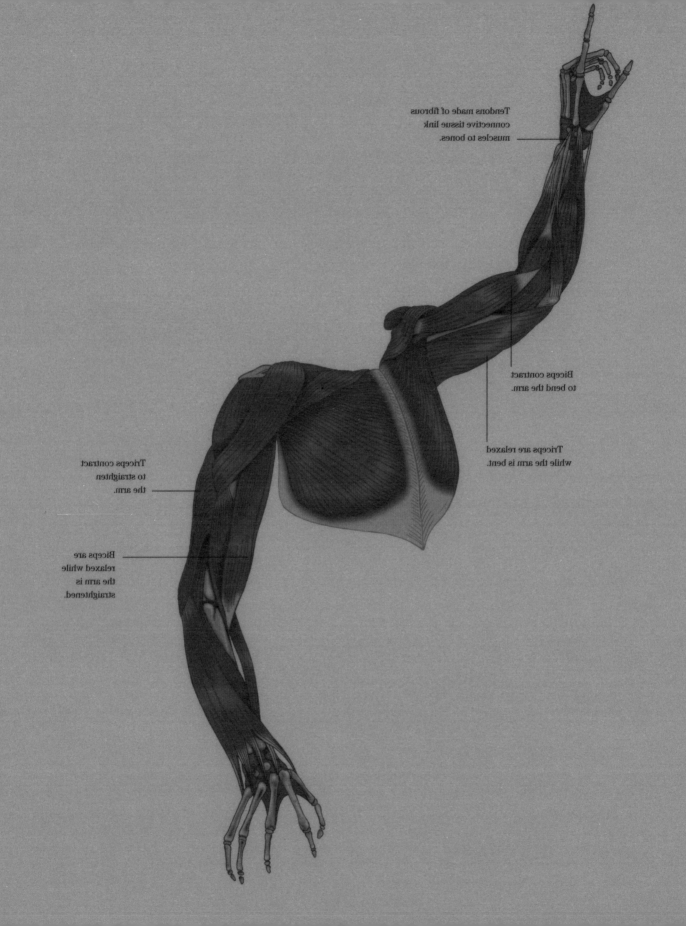

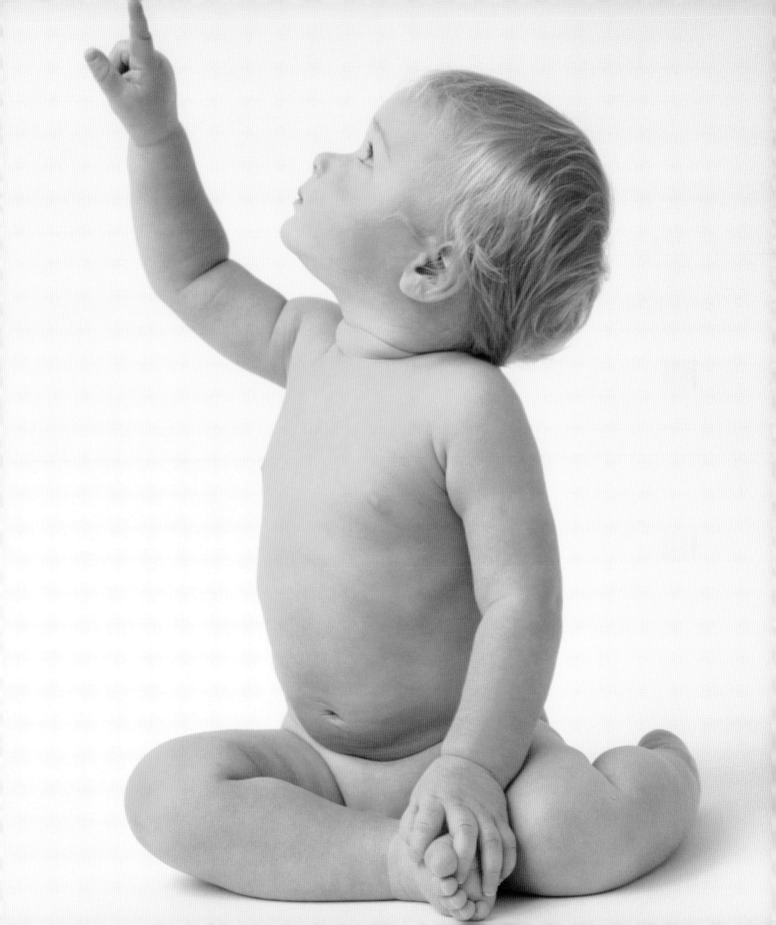

flexibility

During the early months, when her bones are still rather soft and bendable, a baby enjoys a remarkable degree of body flexibility. She can perform odd movements and adopt strange postures that only an adult contortionist could hope to achieve. She can, for example, grab her own toes and pull her foot toward her mouth.

Baby massage has become increasingly popular and it is claimed that, by giving your baby a gentle daily massage, you can increase her flexibility as well as improve her blood circulation, increase coordination and help the development of good posture. The truth is that the natural growth of a healthy infant should provide all the physical improvements that are necessary. As babies adore physical contact a daily massage can only do good, but it is unlikely to increase her natural flexibility. As the baby grows older, the very flexible, cartilaginous parts of her skeleton harden to bone and her infant flexibility is reduced as the body becomes stronger and increasingly mobile.

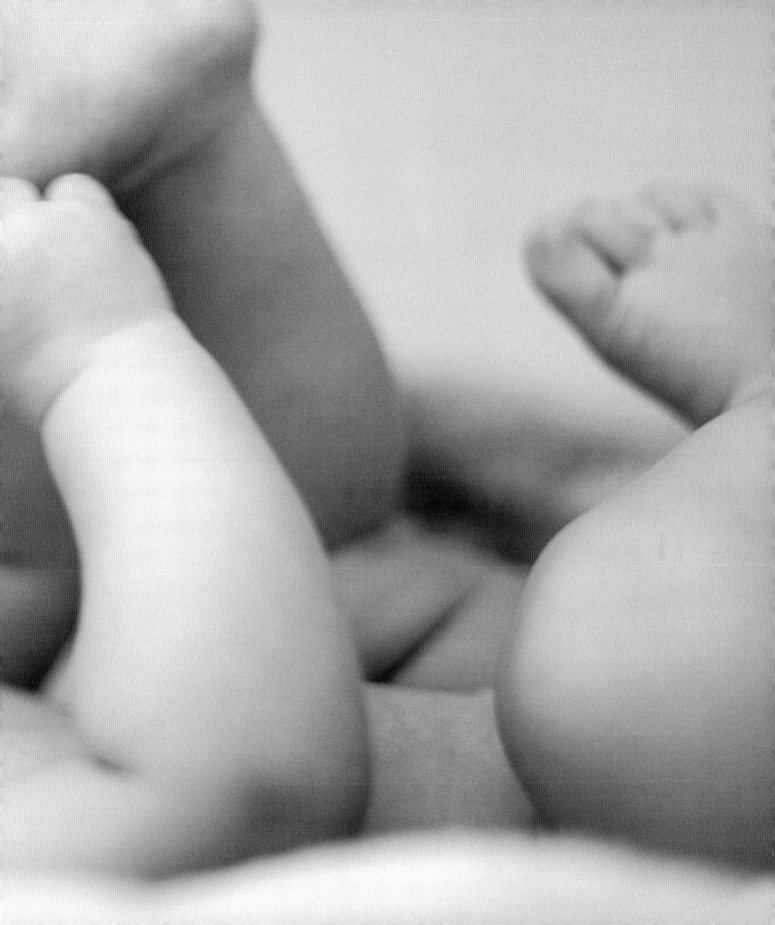

the hands

When a baby is born his small hands are incapable of precise movements. Apart from his powerful inborn grasp reflex (see A baby's reflexes, page 23), he does little with his fingers other than clench them tight. Soon, however, his hands are capable of reaching out and grasping hold of small objects that catch his attention. The next, vital stage is reaching out, grasping and then pulling the held object to the mouth for examination. Later on, his fingers are capable of more delicate, more precise actions in addition to the primitive power grasp.

early movement

For the first few weeks following birth a baby's hands stay clenched most of the time. Then, at about six weeks, he tries pulling at one hand with the other. At eight weeks, he starts to experiment with opening and closing his fingers, and if he has a hanging toy dangling above him, he hits out at it to make it move.

palmar grasp

When a baby is 12 weeks old, his hand movements are more controlled as he hits out at objects near to him. He plays more with his hands now, exploring them to find out how they work. At 16 weeks, he tries out two-handed grasping and gathering objects toward him. The baby's movements are still clumsy, grasping an object with his whole hand rather than just his fingers, but the range of hand actions is developing all the time. By 20 weeks, his grasp is stronger and more efficient. There is a tendency to bring objects up to the mouth and investigate them with the lips and tongue.

clasping and letting go

As a baby enters his seventh month, his hand actions are advanced enough for him to start playing with wooden blocks and other similar toys. He can also move a held object from one hand to the other and back again, and can let go of the object voluntarily. At eight months, he extends his hand-to-mouth actions to attempt self-feeding. When given a drink, he may clasp the mug with his hands, struggling to hold it up to his mouth by himself, usually with little success. This is the stage when dexterity advances by leaps and bounds.

pincer movement

By now a baby has discovered the fun of clapping his hands together and the first sign of individual finger action appears, usually pointing using just the forefinger. This heralds the use of individual fingers and the major step of employing the thumb-and-forefinger precision grip that enables a baby to pick up and hold small objects with some accuracy – a stage most commonly reached in the tenth month after birth.

By the end of his first year, a baby is able to turn the pages of a simple book, clasp objects firmly, use his pincerlike precision grip more and more skillfully, pile up toys and knock them down again, and feed himself with a spoon. During the second year of life, all these manual skills are refined and developed, with more and more accurate control appearing week by week.

baby fingerprints

Fingerprints appear on the hands of babies even before they are born. Somewhere between the third and the fifth month inside the womb, the tiny fingers of the fetus start to show patterns of ridges. These are unique to each individual and once formed will stay the same for the entire life span. Even though the fingerprints enlarge as the hands grow bigger, the complex patterns of ridges do not change.

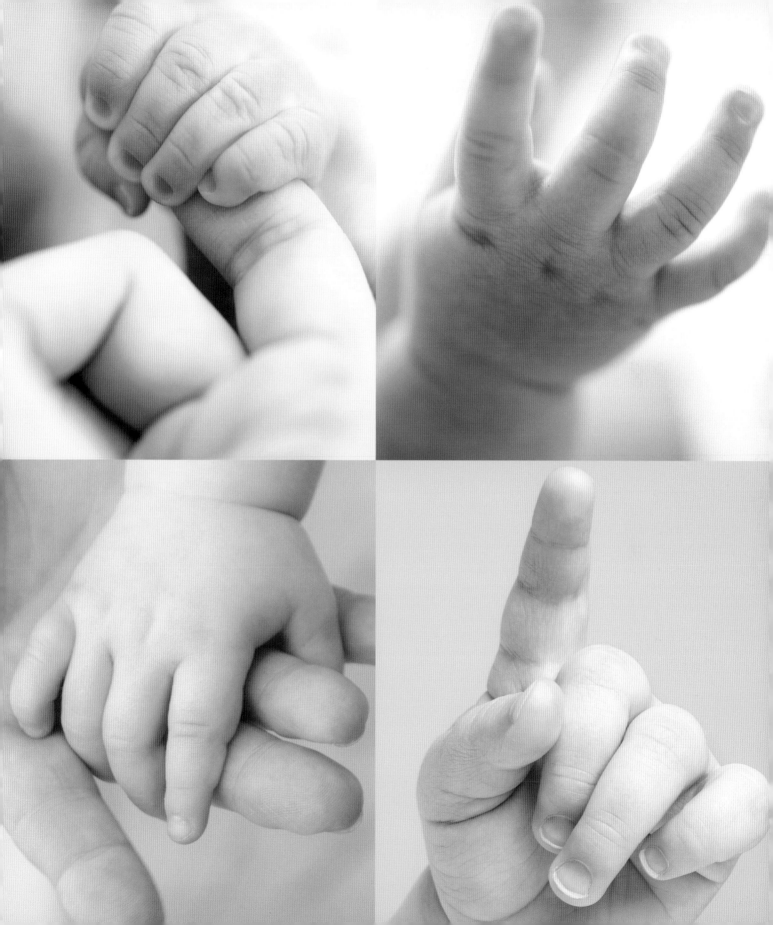

hand activity

A baby goes through a complicated sequence of "hand phases" as she advances through the first few years of life. It is as if a pendulum swings back and forth from left to right, first favoring one hand and then the other. By the time the pendulum stops swinging the child settles on one hand and becomes either right- or left-handed for the rest of her life. But while it is swinging back and forth, matters are not at all clear about where it will finally stop.

early tendencies

If offered an object at three months, a baby usually holds out both hands at the same time. Arm movements are not at all precise and first one hand and then the other becomes dominant. At this early phase, therefore, there is no left or right bias. When offered an object at four months, a baby reaches out with one hand and, in the majority of cases, it is the left hand. Careful studies have revealed that the left bias at this phase of development has no bearing on adult hand preference. Indeed, this left bias disappears at six months and there is no strongly preferred hand.

pendulum swings

At around seven months the pendulum swings to the right. A baby still experiments, first with one hand and then with the other, but the overall bias is now toward right-handedness. The right bias disappears at eight months, however, and the baby uses left and right hands equally. The pendulum swings back to the left again at nine months, by which time the baby is more strongly left-handed than before. At 10 months there is yet another shift and the right hand once again becomes the dominant one.

At some time around 11 months, a baby may switch back to the left hand but, for the majority, it is still the right hand that dominates. This situation persists until the end of the first year of life and one might assume that handedness is now fixed for life. But this is not the case.

further experiments

Approaching 20 months confusion returns and a baby uses both hands again with no clear sign of hand bias. At the end of her second year, a baby's right hand regains the dominant role once more. Then, between the ages of two and a half and three and a half, a toddler goes through one last confused phase, with no particular hand dominating. After that, at about four years of age, the growing child at long last settles down to either a right or left bias. This preference grows stronger as the years pass and, by the time the child is eight years old, she arrives at her permanent handedness and is either right- or left-handed for the rest of her life.

left-handed or right-handed?

At this phase one child out of ten is left-handed and nine out of ten are right-handed. Nobody is certain why human beings have such a strong bias toward right-handedness. We do know from studies of ancient hand axes, however, that the bias has existed for at least 200,000 years, so it is not a modern development.

Some clues come from the way in which an unborn baby lies inside her mother's womb, when she establishes a preferred position toward the end of her pregnancy. The majority lie with their right sides closer to the mother's body surface. This may mean that the right side of the fetus receives more stimulation during pregnancy and becomes more advanced than the left. Anatomically, in the majority of cases, there are more nerves leading to the right side of the body of the fetus than to the left. And, at birth, a newborn baby shows stronger electrical activity on the side of the brain that controls the right side of the body. So it would seem that, from the very beginning, there is a slight bias toward the right.

learning to roll

For many babies the very first method of locomotion is rolling over. If a toy is just out of reach, a baby strains and struggles and then, to his own great surprise, manages to tip his body over, rolling in the direction of the desired object. Once he has discovered that he can do this, it becomes an exciting adventure to repeat over and over again.

front to back

The easier way of rolling – from front to back – can appear very early indeed. About one-third of "rolling babies" manage this maneuver by the end of their third month. Placed on his stomach, a baby starts out by lifting his head up as high as possible, and then tips himself over to one side. As his arm and neck muscles get stronger, so does the tipping action, until one day he finds himself flipping right over on to his back. The next step is using the rolling action deliberately to get closer to something – a toy, a parent or something else that attracts his attention.

back to front

For most babies, the reverse flip – from back to front – usually arrives a little later, at about five months. By the age of six months over 90 percent of babies master both rolling techniques and use them to get around, albeit in a clumsy and highly inefficient manner. A few babies manage the reverse flip first, before the front to back flip, and some do not bother with either, but move straight on to the next phases of sitting and crawling without ever indulging in rolling.

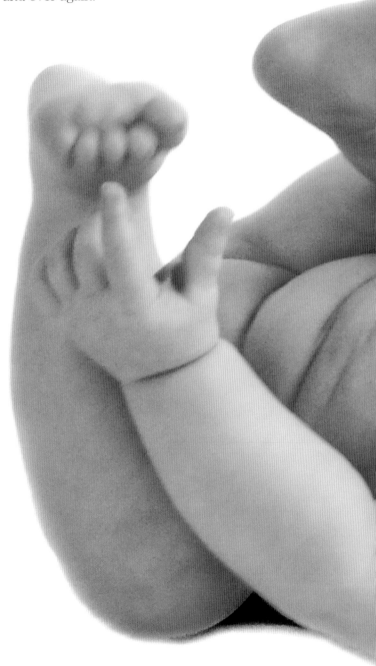

rolling safely

Once a baby starts to roll, it is important for the parent to be extra vigilant when leaving him, even momentarily, on a bed or changing table. This does not mean, however, that rolling should be discouraged. On the contrary, by placing a toy just out of reach it is possible to encourage a baby to exercise his body in this way. Safe rolling is an excellent form of exercise for a baby's limbs and neck muscles. It is a form of infant gymnastics that helps to strengthen muscles and coordinate limb actions.

learning to sit

During the first few months of life, a baby sees the world from an unusual perspective. Most of the time she lies on her back staring up at the ceiling but, whenever her parents cuddle her and hold her in their arms, she views the world the way the rest of us see it, before she returns to observing from ground level.

halfway there

This changes when a baby's neck muscles grow stronger and she can lift her head up a little. Soon, with help from parental hands, she tries to sit up, although she usually slumps back down pretty quickly again. Her muscles are developing slowly and parents must be patient. Soon the baby will have passed a major threshold and will be sitting up unaided.

tripod position

Once a baby has experienced being supported in a sitting posture, at around three months, she will struggle to regain this most interesting position. Eventually she has the strength to heave herself up, but as yet she lacks the balance to retain this wonderful new view of the world for any length of time. So she adopts the "tripod" position, which involves steadying herself with both hands resting on the floor in front of her.

look, no hands!

Somewhere between the ages of four and seven months, nearly all babies manage to sit up by themselves, without any support. With the neck, back and leg muscles all getting stronger, a baby can get up and stay up, much to her delight. The most common age for this important development is five months, but a few late starters do not manage it until eight months old. In addition to enjoying the exciting new view from her sitting posture, a baby is also suddenly free to use her arms and hands. She can reach for things, hold and examine them. Offered suitable toys, she discovers a whole new world of exploration.

and she's off…

Between seven and nine months, a baby is usually able to retain the sitting posture for at least a few minutes but she is about to cross another, even more exciting threshold – that of being able to crawl around on all fours. All she has to do is lean forward from the sitting position and let her hands rest on the floor. Then, balancing on hands and knees, it is only a short move to gain the crawling action and, at long last, off she goes!

learning to crawl

Between the ages of five and eight months, the majority of babies discover the crawl – the first action that makes them efficiently mobile. Other, earlier methods of moving around, such as rolling and bottom-shuffling, could never give a baby a rapid form of locomotion, but crawling on hands and knees can be surprisingly fast and allows the infant to explore the world around him in an exciting new way.

the true crawl

The most primitive form of crawling involves a baby dragging his body forward without raising his underside off the ground. It is a laborious way to progress, however, and soon gives way to the true crawl, where the baby raises his body up and moves forward on hands and knees. This happens at about seven months, and allows the baby to experience the sudden joy of traveling across the floor at speed in search of new and wonderful things to explore and investigate.

The basis of the crawl is not the alternating movement of the hands and feet, but of the hands and knees, the legs being kept bent. As soon as a baby discovers this form of progression, he is sometimes so excited that he crawls backward when the toy he wants is in front of him. It seems that the backward movement comes more easily and a baby has to learn, bit by bit, to direct his body the way he wants to go.

Between the ages of nine months and one year the efficiency of crawling develops rapidly, and some babies achieve a good speed. A baby that develops the habit of doing a great deal of rapid, energetic crawling will, in the process, strengthen his arm, leg and back muscles – all good preparation for the great moment when he finally starts to walk. Toys placed playfully out of reach encourage this active crawling.

variations

The exact age at which a baby begins to crawl varies enormously from infant to infant. About 8 percent of babies start crawling precociously when they are younger than five months. At the other end of the scale, 6 percent are older than 10 months when they first perform this action. A few never crawl – instead they go straight from rolling, bottom-shuffling or slithering to walking, missing out the crawling stage altogether. This is rare but it does sometimes occur.

crawl hazards

A baby displays a remarkably high level of curiosity and once he has started to crawl, he can satisfy this powerful urge in a number of highly dangerous ways. He loves to push his fingers into small holes, such as electric sockets. He is fascinated by the control buttons on the front of the television set and by the wires behind it. He adores pulling downward on low-hanging tablecloths. He loves to crawl inside kitchen cupboards full of cleaning chemicals. And he is especially partial to picking up small, sharp objects and popping them into his mouth. The parental precautions needed to avoid such hazards and baby-proof the house are obvious enough.

learning to stand

Standing alone and unaided is an important milestone for a growing baby. The age at which this happens varies from child to child, but is most likely to occur when the infant is about eight months old. Roughly a quarter of them manage it slightly earlier and some are late starters, with 5 percent of babies not standing free until they are over a year old.

standing alone

The triumph of standing alone does not come suddenly, but passes through three stages. Initially, a baby stands while being held by a parent. In this position, she can try out the strength of her legs and get a feel for what it is like to be upright. If the parent relaxes his hold slightly, he feels the baby's legs start to sag and knows that she is not yet ready. Having developed a taste for the novel sensation of being vertical, the baby now crawls toward a piece of furniture – a chair or a table – and starts to haul herself up. Once upright, she pauses to survey the world from her newly elevated position and then promptly collapses backward, sitting down with a bump. Undeterred, she keeps repeating this activity until, one glorious day, she manages to stay standing alone without falling down – the final stage in this challenging journey.

the joints

There are 230 joints in the human body. Some are fixed and allow no movement, but the majority are primarily concerned with altering the posture of the human body. They are unable to operate efficiently in a newborn baby because the body systems that use them (skeleton, muscles and nervous system) are not yet strongly developed, and this leaves the infant helpless. Within the first two years, however, all these systems stir into action and, by his second birthday, a toddler's joints all work to great effect.

fibrous joints

These connect bones without allowing any movement. The bones of the skull and the pelvic girdle are rigid with the different sections held together by fibrous joints. These joints also develop in the vertebral column when the bones there start to fuse as part of the growing process.

cartilaginous joints

These are joints in which the bones are attached to one another by cartilage. They permit very little movement. The ribs and the vertebrae come into this category.

synovial joints

Synovial joints are the truly mobile ones, involved in all the major actions of the body. Wherever two bones meet and have some degree of movement there is the risk of friction and this is reduced by the presence of more flexible cartilage. The bones are capped with this cartilage, providing a buffer between the two hard surfaces. As an additional aid, a protective membrane secretes a synovial liquid, which lubricates all the moving parts of the joints. There are seven different types of synovial joint:

The ball-and-socket joint gives the greatest freedom of movement. A baby has four of these – two at the shoulders and two at the hips. At the hips, the rounded end of the upper leg bone, the femur, fits into a deep socket in the pelvic girdle. At the shoulders, in a similar way, the upper arm bone, the humerus, fits into a socket in the shoulder blade, or scapula. This shoulder socket is shallower than the hip socket, giving the arm greater range of movements than the leg, or any other joint in the body. However, with this advantage comes the risk that the shoulder joint can be dislocated more easily than the hip joint.

The ellipsoid joint is similar to the ball-and-socket joint, but with less freedom of movement. The wrist has an ellipsoid joint, as do the fingers at the point where they meet the palm of the hand. These joints allow flexion and extension and rocking from side to side. If these two

elements are combined they create a crude form of rotation, but of a much more limited kind than is possible with the ball-and-socket joint.

The saddle joint is a highly mobile joint, allowing movement back and forth and up and down, with one concave bone-ending fitting into another concavity. The ankle and the base of the thumb have saddle joints.

The hinge joint allows only one plane of action – extension and flexion – up and down, or back and forth. The elbow has a hinge joint.

The condylar joint is similar to the hinge joint but allows rotation in addition to the basic bending action. The knee has a condylar joint. Because the mechanism of the knee is so complex, and essential to the uniquely human action of walking erect, this joint has an extra protective device: small, fluid-filled sacs called bursae that act as shock absorbers.

The plane joint allows very little movement and is found between the joints of the toes. It may also be called a gliding joint, in which case the bones slide past one another when movement occurs.

The pivot joint allows rotation around an axis. This is found between two neck bones – the atlas and the axis – where it permits rotation of the head. The forearms also have pivot joints, with the radius and ulna twisting around each other.

learning to walk

The solo walk sets the human baby apart from all other young mammals. There are over 4,000 species of mammals alive on the planet today, but only one of them is a true bipedal walker. Kangaroos may be bipedal, but they do not walk, they hop. Apes and bears may stagger for a few steps on their hind legs, but only humans spend much of their adult lives standing vertically and putting one foot boldly in front of the other.

the vertical world

We tend to take this very much for granted and yet it is one of our unique qualities, and the baby's first experience of this form of locomotion is a major event in her life, leaving behind the "all fours" world she shared with other young mammals and at last joining the curiously vertical, uniquely human society.

an important milestone

Learning to walk is a huge milestone in a child's life and a big step toward independence. Most babies learn to walk unaided between the ages of 12 and 15 months, with girls slightly ahead of boys. The first steps are the culmination of months of effort (and a fair amount of trial and error) as a baby develops strength, balance and coordination, starting with head control and gradually progressing through the body to the legs.

a natural progression

The ability to walk survives the most restrictive regimes. Even in tribes and societies where infants are strapped to boards and carried by adults for long periods of time, the babies may reach their developmental milestones later than most children, but still eventually manage to walk, nevertheless. This shows that there is an amazing maturing process taking place in each baby that is programmed before birth.

six stages of walking

The very first signs that a baby is programmed for walking appear only a few days after birth. Supported by parental hands so that his feet just touch the ground, a newborn baby kicks out in a vigorous way as if trying to progress forward. These are automatic, reflex actions and cannot be controlled or modified by the baby (see A baby's reflexes, page 23). They disappear after about two months but are a clear indication that the action of bipedal walking is deeply embedded in the human brain.

stage two

This stage, from about two months, shows the growing baby quite incapable of performing any sort of prewalking actions. Held by parents now, with his feet just touching the ground, he simply sags at the knees. The early kicking actions have gone.

stage three

At about three months, or slightly later, instead of sagging at the knees when held over a hard surface, a baby's legs stiffen and attempt to support his body. As the weeks pass this "parentally supported" phase shows improvement, with the baby's legs becoming stronger and better able to keep his body erect.

stage four

Typically between six and nine months comes the "heaving upright" phase in which an active infant does his best to pull himself up on to his legs by grabbing hold of some convenient piece of furniture. Once he has managed this, he proudly surveys his new domain for a while and then promptly collapses with a bump, back down on to the ground. Unless he hits something on the way, this setback does not deter the baby for long. The sensation of being higher up in the world is irresistible and he soon heaves himself up once more, gradually becoming accustomed to the new sensation of supporting his body weight on his legs.

stage five

This stage is true forward walking with the aid of parental hands, and is usually first seen between the ages of nine and 12 months. It consists of a few faltering steps followed by a loss of balance. The parent prevents the baby falling over, but the baby finds these initial failures highly frustrating. He now knows exactly what he wants to do and is upset that he is too clumsy to achieve his goal. But he perseveres and each stumbling progression becomes a little more controlled than the last until the great moment arrives when he strides out alone to walk a few first unaided paces across the room.

stage six

A baby takes his first few tentative steps with arms held high and elbows bent as an aid to balance. The steps are wide apart, uneven in length and unsteady, but after a few months the movements are far more controlled and the arms are no longer held up for balance. By 18 months most toddlers are confident walkers and tumbles are rare.

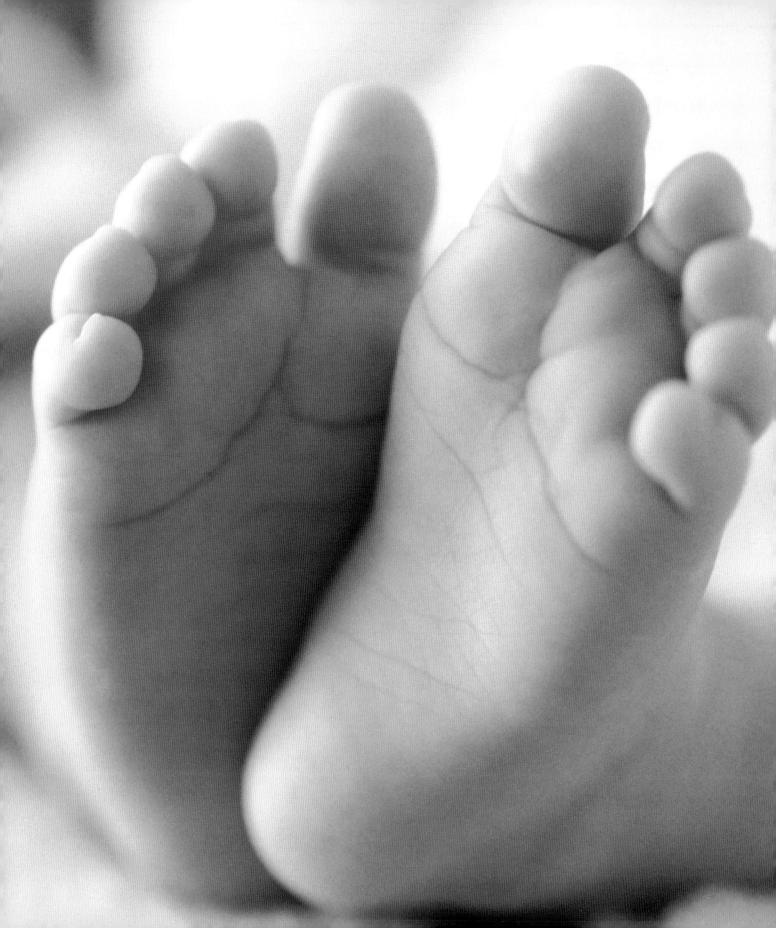

the feet

At birth, a newborn baby's feet are one-third of their adult length. At the age of one year they are nearly half their adult size. Apart from this size difference, a baby's feet differ from those of the adult in several ways. They are heavily padded with fat, making them much softer and rounder than adult feet. They are also much more flexible, as the bones inside them are still developing from cartilage to bone. And they tend to turn inward, giving the baby a pigeon-toed look. This last quality results from the fetus having been squashed up inside her mother's womb for so long before birth. By the time a baby is starting to walk, however, these newborn qualities are far less marked.

straight feet

The inward-turned feet of the newborn slowly straighten out as the months pass. Some parents are worried when they see their toddlers attempting to walk with a bandy-legged, pigeon-toed gait, but this is perfectly normal and is adjusted naturally as a child learns to walk less clumsily. There is no point in attempting to hurry the process.

baby shoes

Many years ago, parents were taught that, because toddlers had wobbly ankles and flat feet, they needed special shoes to help them walk. Stiff, high-top, hard-sole leather shoes were recommended to enable babies to walk sooner. However, modern research has found that toddlers are not, in fact, flat-footed. When played back in slow motion, video recordings of young children making their very first attempts at walking show that they use a heel-to-toe action similar to that seen in walking adults. Also, their ankles are capable of providing excellent balance. All that is needed when learning to walk, therefore, is a period of practice as the toddler learns how to perform this new kind of locomotion, and her foot muscles and ligaments toughen up from repeated use.

going barefoot

Studies of children growing up in shoeless, tribal cultures show that fewer foot problems are experienced than in countries where wearing shoes is the norm. The more a toddler is allowed to walk about with bare feet, the better the natural growth and development of her feet as the months pass. The barefoot toddler develops stronger and more coordinated muscles than the carefully shod one. Shoes should be worn, not for walking inside the family home, but for protection against harsh surfaces and against the elements when the infant is out and about.

climbing

Between the ages of seven and 12 months, a baby masters fast crawling sufficiently to want to explore new possibilities, and one activity that appeals is climbing. This proves an exhilarating experience, taking the infant literally to new heights (of which he seems fearless). The sudden arrival of more adventurous pursuits and investigations has its own hazards, however. The active baby may thrill to the novelty of unfamiliar experiences, but at the same time he is as unaware of what can go wrong, and therefore unprepared for any kind of danger.

allure of stairs

For some reason a stairway is a powerful draw for the fast-crawling baby. The hands-and-knees posture of the infant seems ideally suited to clambering up stairs at top speed. And the intrepid climber, never having fallen downstairs in his short life, is completely fearless as he ascends higher and higher. Now an awkward moment arrives. The baby, suddenly feeling that this particular climbing game is over, is faced with the problem of getting down again. Turning around and coming down headfirst is a dangerous option with the center of balance all wrong. Instead he needs the help of an adult in coming down backward.

standing and reaching up

For a baby of seven to 12 months, any object placed out of reach has a special attraction. If it is too high, he experiments with clambering up toward it, raising an arm as far as possible and then grabbing at it. This is often done clumsily, with the result that the object in question tumbles down on top of the baby. Curiosity knows no bounds at this stage, and it is remarkable just how many dangers there are lurking around an ordinary house, that can do harm to the more adventurous baby.

learning safely

For reckless babies, one solution is to install a baby gate to prevent access to the stairway. These work well at first, but can easily become a challenge for the baby – an obstacle to be overcome by risky clambering. A more drastic measure is the large playpen in which the demon crawler is confined and from which he has no escape. Stocked with soft toys, this will keep the crawler happy for a while and is useful as a brief resort when something urgent requires the attention of the mother, but eventually the confined space begins to frustrate the baby's inquisitive nature.

A baby thrives in a crawl-safe playroom, in which the entire area is hazard-free but offers plenty of room for him to exercise newfound skills. If he has a few small objects to climb over, placed on a soft carpet, he has the chance to experience the failure moment of falling without harming himself. He has to learn caution somehow and "safe accidents" are the only pleasant way to do this.

climbers and nonclimbers

Strangely, climbing does not have appeal for all infants. There is enormous variation in the juvenile urge to ascend. Some babies ignore high places altogether, some are mildly interested and others seem to be obsessed with them. The last group requires special watching. One father was startled to hear his toddler, not yet two years old, call out "Daddy" from just behind him. The reason this shocked him was because, at the time, he was repairing the roof of the family house. To his horror he realized that the infant had climbed up a tall ladder and was now perched on the roof behind him!

staying healthy

safe and well

A newborn baby has a degree of natural protection from the diseases that lurk in the outside world. In addition to a limited built in immune mechanism, he also acquires immunity from his mother's blood while he is in the womb. If he is breast-fed, he gains further immunity from his mother's milk, which is rich in antibodies. This is especially true during the first few days of his life in the outside world, when he receives the premilk, or colostrum.

Unfortunately this maternal protection does not last forever, but merely serves as an emergency defense during the earliest months, when the baby has not yet had the chance to obtain immunity in any other way. From this time on, his immune system develops defenses of its own through exposure to mild infections, which helps create the antibodies that protect him when something worse comes along (see A baby's defense system, page 96).

vaccination

In addition to a baby's developing immune system, there are a number of protective vaccinations that can help the infant to resist diseases that pose a particular threat. A baby usually makes five or six vaccination visits to the doctor during the first two years of life. It is true that some babies suffer minor side effects from vaccination, such as a mild fever, but it is generally recognized that the benefits of immunization easily outweigh the risks.

A vaccine is prepared by weakening or killing the disease-causing bacteria or viruses and then introducing them, by mouth or injection, into a baby's body. There they act as if they are the real disease and cause the defense system to produce protective antibodies. But they do this without causing the dangerous illness that usually goes with the disease if caught in the normal way. Once the baby produces the antibodies, these provide immunity for a long time.

multi-vaccines

Recently there has been some argument about the safety of new multi-vaccinations in which an infant is given five different disease protections with a single injection. This five-in-one immunization is given at eight, 12 and 16 weeks of age, and protects the baby against diphtheria, tetanus, whooping cough, *Haemophilus influenzae* type B (Hib) and polio. Critics of this procedure claim that there is a danger of overloading the baby's immune system, but medical authorities insist that a large number of clinical trials show that there is little or no risk of this. In addition to the five-in-one jab, it is also possible to provide protection against various other diseases, such as hepatitis B, with an injection given shortly after the birth of the baby, and measles, mumps and rubella (MMR), given later, at the age of 12 to 15 months.

parental protection

The human infant is remarkably resilient, heals quickly and has a good immune system but, despite this, he takes a long time to develop either the sensitivity or the necessary motor skills to keep him safe within his environment. Modern cities and buildings are full of dangers that did not exist in prehistoric times, such as the many toxic household products, and infants have no natural reactions to protect them from such artificial hazards.

A baby must learn to avoid injury by experience, therefore minor bumps and bruises may cause frantic crying but in the long run they become part of the learning process by which a growing child acquires a greater dexterity and "native cunning" in dealing with the hazards of his environment. The trick is for the parent to find as many ways as possible of reducing the dangers present in an otherwise rich environment, so that the infant can enjoy full expression with the minimum of risk.

signs of illness

A baby spends much of her early life suffering from minor ailments as she builds up resistance to a host of general complaints, and she is remarkably good at letting her parents know whenever she is feeling ill. If she is crying and all the obvious causes have been investigated – hunger, heat, cold, wetness, loneliness and fear – then the chances are that she is in pain or is unwell.

Among the typical signs of illness are a rise or fall in temperature, vomiting and diarrhea, a withdrawn and unresponsive look, a cold sweat, rapid breathing that goes on for a long time and a baby that is "floppy." If symptoms persist, parents should seek the advice of a doctor.

snuffling babies

A baby can catch a cold just like an adult but, sadly for her, she cannot reach for a handkerchief to blow her nose or wipe it dry. In fact, babies get cold viruses more often than adults – this is a normal part of the development of their immune system. Despite years of study, science has failed to find a cure for this most common of ailments, and a baby has no choice but to wait it out like anyone else. She needs a little more help than an adult, however. With a blocked nose, her biggest problem arrives at feeding time when she tries to suck milk and breathe through her mouth at the same time, which could result in low food intake.

feverish babies

Fever occurs when the body overheats, usually because of the body's response to an infection. Fever, in itself, is nothing to worry about. However, it is a signal that the infant is battling against an intruder, and if the feverish condition persists or the baby has a febrile fit, a doctor should be consulted.

colic

Not all babies suffer from colic – it affects one or two in every 10 infants – but for those who do, symptoms usually start within a week or so of birth and last for as long as three months or more. A colicky baby cries or screams on and off for hours, almost always in the early evening, and quite often with her legs drawn up to her tummy as if in considerable pain. The causes of colic are unknown, although it is thought to be either a digestive problem or one of tension in the immature nervous system.

allergies

Some babies suffer from an overactive immune system that reacts toward a normally harmless substance as if it were a dangerous invader. When this happens, a baby's immune system starts releasing chemicals to counteract the invader. Having no real invaders to fight (bacteria or viruses) the immune response irritates the infant's body instead. It takes some time for allergic responses to build up and a baby does not show symptoms at first. After some months, symptoms may begin to appear, such as sneezing, congestion, a runny nose, itchy or watery eyes, a dry cough, skin rashes or intestinal problems. More serious symptoms, requiring medical attention, are wheezing and swelling, especially of the mouth and tongue.

For the problem to arise, the allergic infant has to come into close contact with the substance, called an allergen, by touching it, breathing it, eating it or having it injected. Among the most common allergens are woollen clothing, down or feather pillows, laundry detergent containing bleach, perfumed soap and chemical sprays for furniture. Other culprits include certain kinds of food, some drugs, insects, pet animal dandruff and dust mites. It is extremely difficult to pinpoint the specific cause in each case. Why most babies escape these problems while others are plagued by them is still not clear.

a baby's defense system

While a baby is in the womb, some of his mother's antibodies cross the placenta and these help protect him from diseases and infections. Although this protection only lasts a few weeks, it receives an extra boost through breast-feeding, since breast milk also contains vital antibodies. Sooner or later, however, a baby becomes less reliant on his mother and must develop his own forms of resistance.

first lines of defense

Infectious microorganisms surround us all the time, and it is amazing how well equipped even the youngest baby is to deal with them. Any virus, bacterium or fungal organism that tries to invade his body has to cross a series of defense lines, and the skin is the first of these. If foreign invaders manage to break through, a baby's body mounts an inflammatory response, releasing chemicals such as histamine, which enlarge the blood vessels and attract white blood cells that overwhelm invading microorganisms at the site of infection. Other early defenders include antibacterial body fluids such as saliva, tears and stomach acid, while hairs and mucus defend the respiratory system.

lymphatic system

The immune system depends on the recognition of foreign antigens. The adenoids and tonsils at the back of a baby's nose and throat play an important part in the destruction of invading organisms – especially since children are particularly prone to nasal and throat infections. These organs form part of the lymphatic system, a network of channels and organs conducting lymph (immune system fluid) around a baby's body.

white blood cells

Lymph contains the defensive white blood cells, of which there are two main types – macrophages, which destroy foreign bodies, and lymphocytes, which create antibodies to provide a baby with lasting immunity to infection.

Lymphocytes mature in the thymus gland, where they are exposed to hormones that help them develop an ability to target particular disease-carrying pathogens. Because of its importance in helping to strengthen the immune system during the first years of life, a baby's thymus is large in comparison to that of an adult.

Lymph moves along the lymph vessels and returns to the bloodstream. As it passes through the lymph nodes (which occur mainly in the neck, armpits and groin), pathogens are filtered out and destroyed by white blood cells. During an infection the lymph nodes may swell up and become tender.

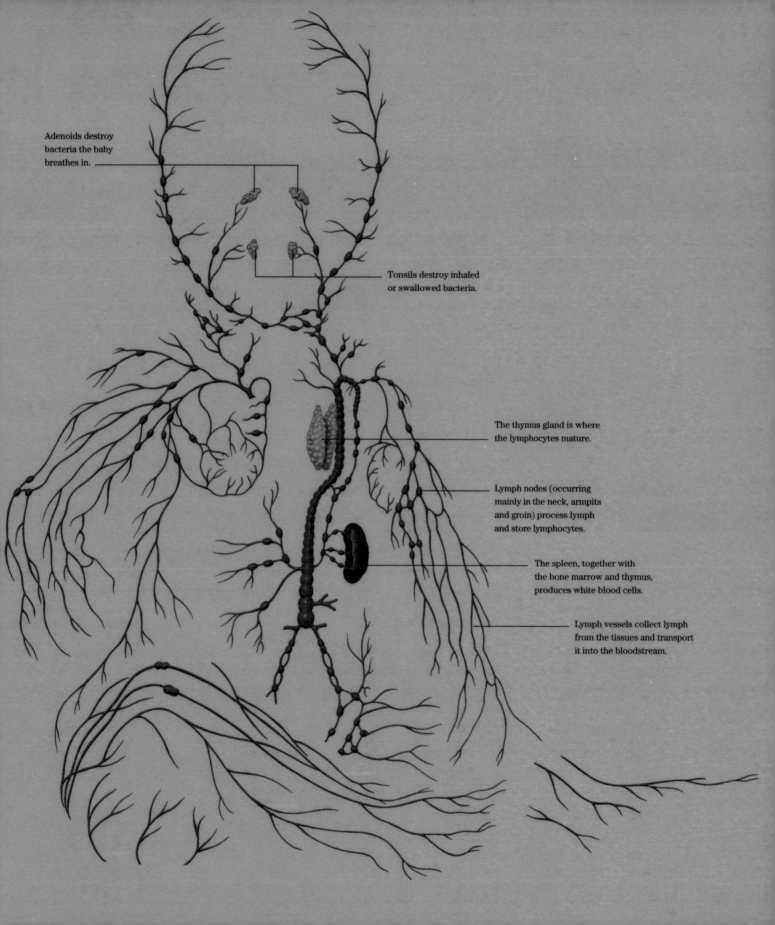

Adenoids destroy
bacteria the baby
breathes in.

Tonsils destroy inhaled
or swallowed bacteria.

The thymus gland is where
the lymphocytes mature.

Lymph nodes (occurring
mainly in the neck, armpits
and groin) process lymph
and store lymphocytes.

The spleen, together with
the bone marrow and thymus,
produces white blood cells.

Lymph vessels collect lymph
from the tissues and transport
it into the bloodstream.

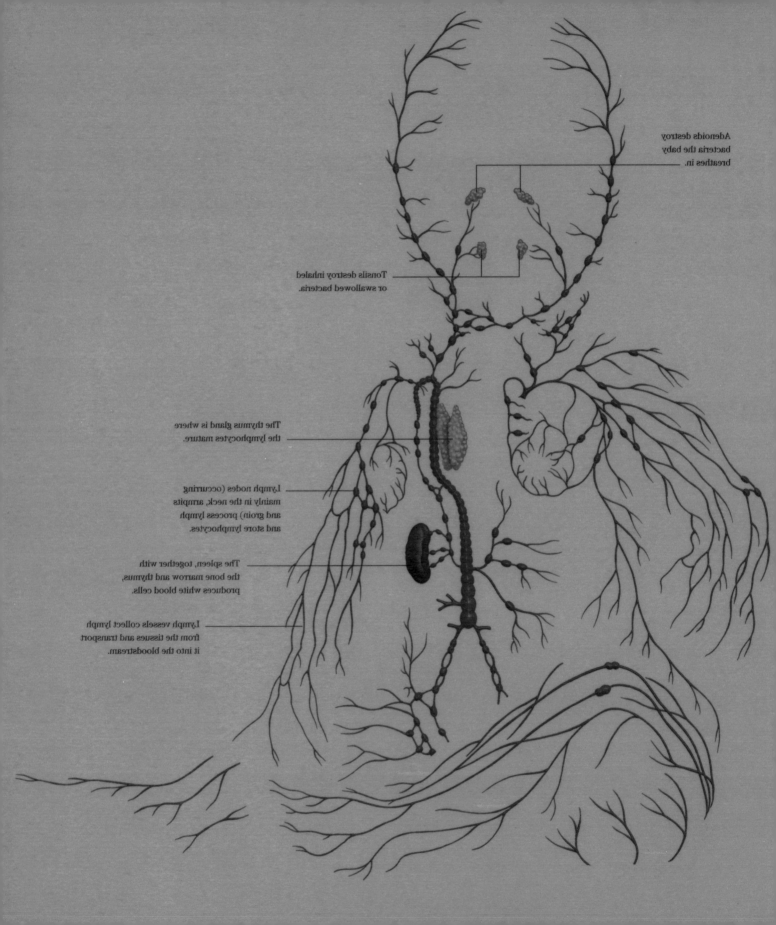

Adenoids destroy
bacteria the baby
breathes in.

Tonsils destroy inhaled
or swallowed bacteria.

The thymus gland is where
the lymphocytes mature.

Lymph nodes (occurring
mainly in the neck, armpits
and groin) process lymph
and store lymphocytes.

The spleen, together with
the bone marrow and thymus,
produces white blood cells.

Lymph vessels collect lymph
from the tissues and transport
it into the bloodstream.

first lines of defense
This magnified and colored scan shows a white blood cell macrophage extending tendrils to engulf and destroy bacteria (shown in red).

dealing with waste

Removal of waste from the body in the form of feces and urine is as important as drinking and feeding. Right from the start, a baby's digestive system is programmed to take what it needs to fuel body activities and growth, and then to discard the surplus and unwanted matter. This discarding process is uncontrolled for many months and demands major assistance from the parents, with seemingly endless diaper changing and skin cleaning.

how it works

The digestive system is essentially a long, muscle-lined tube through which food passes from a baby's mouth to her anus. The food is moved along by the expansion and contraction of muscles, and as it passes through the system it is broken down by the action of substances such as saliva in the mouth and gastric juices in the stomach. Essential nutrients – vitamins, minerals, fats, proteins and carbohydrates – are absorbed into the tube wall, while waste products are eliminated as feces. The liver, pancreas and gallbladder produce the enzymes that aid the absorption of these essential nutrients, which are then distributed through the baby's body via the bloodstream. Meanwhile, the kidneys filter the blood, eliminating waste products in the form of urine.

first bowel movement

Within a day or so of being born a baby accomplishes her first bowel movement. The feces produced at this time are of a special kind, called meconium. This is odorless, blackish green in color and consists of digested detritus from the intestines – a combination of digested mucus from glands in the digestive tract and digested gut-lining cells, shed from the walls of the intestines.

Once a baby starts excreting milk residue from breast- or bottle-feeding, the dark color of the meconium gradually lightens until it becomes a pale yellow-brown. The feces of a breast-fed baby are soft, with little odor. They appear several times a day and may be yellow, yellow and green, or green in color. This color variation reflects the fact that the baby's new digestive system is still settling down to its complicated task.

daily routine

A baby usually defecates shortly after waking and again about half an hour after feeding. She urinates frequently – about every 20 minutes for a newborn baby and roughly every hour at six months. Before she has bladder and bowel control she cannot influence the precise moment at which she urinates or defecates, but parents who get to know the approximate timings can anticipate the events and be ready for them.

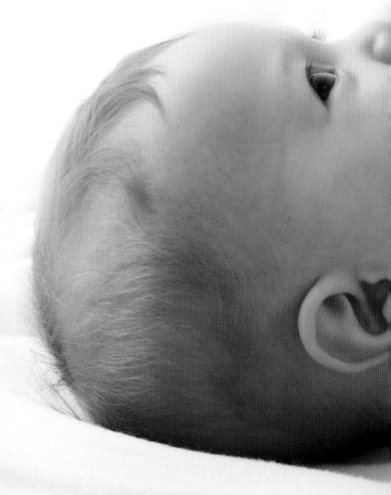

the body's filter system
This colored X-ray shows how arteries branch into a network of smaller blood vessels within a kidney, allowing the kidney to filter waste products from the blood and excrete them as urine.

body controls

Every time the body performs an action, two things happen. The brain sends messages to the muscles telling them to get moving. At the same time the body's self-controlling system goes into operation to ensure that the new outburst of activity has its full support. The autonomic nervous system operates the controls and the somatic nervous system deals with the movements.

autonomic nervous system

When the body is resting it conserves energy. When it becomes active the body calls on its reserves of energy to ensure that a task is performed efficiently. It is the job of the autonomic nervous system to keep the body fine-tuned to its moment-by-moment level of activity. It does this by operating two opposing forces – what we could call the brake and the accelerator. When the brake is on, all the energetic elements slow right down and the body relaxes. When the accelerator is pressed, everything suddenly speeds up and all the support systems swing into action, as the body tenses to perform the rapid movements being demanded. This accelerator is called the sympathetic nervous system, and when it becomes active it floods the body with adrenaline. The braking that slows everything down again is controlled by the parasympathetic system. At any one time, one of these two systems is dominant, as the body swings back and forth between the rest and relaxation of the parasympathetic and the vigorous activity of the sympathetic.

sympathetic system

The sympathetic system ensures efficient action in the following ways: it increases the heart rate, pumping more blood around the body and raising the blood pressure; it increases the breathing rate, providing more oxygen; by controlling the dilation and constriction of different blood vessels, it shunts blood from the skin and the gut to the muscles; it increases sweating as a cooling system, anticipating that the body's action may cause it to overheat; it also increases sweating of the palms of the hand as a way of ensuring a better grip in case the anticipated actions become violent; it inhibits urination; and it reduces the watery secretions of the salivary glands and the tear glands, reserving body liquids for more urgent tasks.

parasympathetic system

The parasympathetic system ensures that these changes are put into reverse. The heartbeat slows down and eases the strain on the heart muscles. Less oxygen is needed, so the lungs can relax too. Blood is shunted away from the muscles and back to the skin and the digestive system. Sweating is dramatically reduced and the salivary and tear glands can become more active again.

adrenal glands

There are different levels of body activity, from gentle walking and playing to panic responses when violence threatens. When the body reaches panic level, the adrenal glands move into high gear. The paired adrenals, found just above the kidneys, have several functions, including the all-important secretion of adrenaline whenever danger threatens. The result of this secretion is that the body is rapidly made ready for violent action – either fighting or fleeing. Neither of these is possible for a baby, but he can at least respond to fear with vigorous crying and thrashing of his limbs. A toddler can do more – he can run in panic to his protective parent.

Prolonged fear or prolonged feelings of aggression that, for any reason, cannot find expression in the form of vigorous activity, involving either fleeing or fighting, may create a state of severe stress. The body is geared up for violent muscular activity but none occurs. If this happens time after time, the body's immune system may weaken and therefore be more prone to illness.

body surface

The largest organ of a baby's body is her skin, and it is doubly important to her well-being. It not only acts as the protective covering for all the other organs, but it also has a profound psychological role to play.

the magic of touch

Because it is rich in touch-sensitive nerve endings, the skin is highly responsive to all forms of body contact. The gentle embrace of a mother, the softness of the clothes she puts on her baby, the tender stroking, kissing, cuddling and bathing that she offers, all add up to a massive expression of tactile love, the most ancient form of all.

Studies have shown that adults who were given little touching as babies are more aggressive than those who were regularly cuddled. Research also shows that girls are more sensitive to touch than boys – on average girls just a few hours old react to a weak puff of air against their belly, and squirm and cry more than boys when uncovered. Other investigators found that plenty of skin contact produces babies that cry less and are generally healthier. It has even been suggested that babies who receive more cuddling and handling may be more intelligent in later life, because all that early touch experience helps to stimulate brain development.

skin quality

A baby's skin is thinner than that of an adult, less oily, less pigmented, less sweaty and less resistant to toxins and bacterial infection. It takes several years for her to develop these features more strongly, and before that happens she obviously needs careful parental protection. The outermost layer of the skin, the epidermis, is not only thin but also more fragile, with the cells less tightly bound together. This means that blisters and sore patches can form more easily. The dermis, the layer that lies just below the epidermis, is four times thinner than that of an adult, and contains fewer collagen and elastic fibers, making this, too, more fragile.

glandular activity

Although a newborn baby is well equipped with sweat glands, the nervous system that controls and regulates these glands is not yet fully operative. As a result, she cannot use these glands for efficient cooling when she starts to overheat. For this reason a baby is at particular risk in very hot weather. Her other skin glands – the sebaceous glands that produce the sebum, which gives skin its oily quality – only start to become active as the months pass. Even then, their output is far below that of an adult and this remains the case throughout childhood. They are active enough, however, to give a baby her appealing personal scent, a scent that is unique to each baby and that can be identified by her mother (see also Bonding, page 31).

skin care

The skin of an infant, being far more delicate, vulnerable and sensitive than that of an adult, needs special care. Diaper rash is the most common form of skin complaint and is caused by not replacing wet diapers quickly enough. Stale urine creates ammonia that irritates the skin and prevents the skin surface from resisting infection. The condition is worsened by contact with bacteria from feces. In addition, the rubbing of the wet surfaces on the skin causes soreness. Bathing in warm water is both cleansing and comforting and while giving the baby a cleaner skin surface, it also provides valuable moments of tactile intimacy with her mother.

communication

crying

During his first year, before communication with words is possible, a baby's only hope of summoning help is to let out a piercing cry. Crying is an ancient alarm call that humans share with many other animals, and it produces a powerful parental response. At first, the baby's cry is a nonspecific signal, telling his parents he is unhappy but not the reason why. As time passes, parents can relate the different kinds of crying to different types of distress.

early crying

The first time a baby cries is usually immediately after the birth, as an expression of shock at the sudden change of environment. Instead of being worried, most parents respond with a broad grin of pleasure at the knowledge that their baby's lungs are working efficiently. He cries most frequently during the first three months following birth, after which regular crying tails off. At around six weeks, his tear ducts develop sufficiently to produce his first tears.

what makes a baby cry?

There are seven reasons why babies cry: pain, discomfort, hunger, loneliness, overstimulation, understimulation or frustration. A sensitive parent soon tells one type of crying from another. Pain is usually expressed with sharp, piercing cries. A baby has no clear idea what is wrong, and cannot distinguish between a minor and a major hurt, so needs to attract a parent quickly. He often stops crying when comforted and continues only if in acute pain. Persistent crying may indicate colic (see Signs of illness, page 95).

A baby cries in discomfort when he soils himself, is too hot or too cold, or if his delicate skin is in contact with a rough surface. Cries often start quietly and get louder as the discomfort escalates. Cries of hunger can be easy to detect by rhythm and the time they occur. When a baby is very hungry, his cries are loud and urgent, with short pauses for breath. The easiest crying to pacify is the sad-sounding, repetitive crying that arises when a baby starts to feel that he has been abandoned. No more is needed here than to be held, or to see a closeup of a smiling parental face. A baby may also cry if he is overstimulated or understimulated. If very tired, these cries are whingey and whiney, and the baby may rub his eyes.

bedtime crying

During the first few months, a baby becomes attached to his mother, and starts to emit a cry of alarm if separated from her. He wants nothing more than to snuggle up close to her, but sleeping arrangements may not allow this. Although the parent knows that, sooner or later, she will return to care for her baby, the baby does not know this. Should the baby's cries of alarm be routinely ignored, somewhere deep in his brain a lack of trust starts to grow. Fears that his mother may never return begin to haunt him and a deep-seated sense of insecurity becomes embedded. No matter how sophisticated this child becomes in later life, he may never attain a true state of self-confidence.

Keeping mother and baby in close proximity to one another for at least the first few months is a simple strategy to avoid such problems. A baby needs to learn to go to sleep by himself, without cuddling or feeding, but this does not mean that the mother has to be totally absent. Keeping a crib in the parent's room for the first few months gives the baby a sense of being near his mother, safe and secure. Once used to this idea, being moved to another room at, say, six months is then far less traumatic for him.

crying toddlers

Cries of frustration usually come later on when a toddler is desperately trying to achieve something but fails. This type of crying increases as the baby begins to flex his muscles and starts to explore his environment, but before he is able to do so efficiently. In extreme cases it may lead to breath holding, where the toddler holds his breath until his face goes from red to blue. He may even lose consciousness. Such bouts often occur during a temper tantrum (see Toddler tantrums, page 165).

smiling

Once a bond develops between a baby and her mother, a new form of communication comes into play. Crying may bring a parent running, but now the baby has to find a way of keeping that parent close. Evolution has given her a special weapon, unique to our species – the human smile. A baby uses this signal as a way of rewarding an adult for staying with her.

the unique smile

Human babies are the only primates to smile at their parents, and this is because they are so helpless, physically. A baby monkey stays close to his mother by clinging to her fur. Human babies cannot do that and desperately need some other way of keeping the mother next to them: the answer is smiling. A mother has an inborn response to this facial expression and cannot help but feel good when she sees her baby smile. In a year's time the toddler is able to talk to her mother and use a whole new system of communication, but even when this happens it does not mean the end of the smile – a basic human signal that lasts a lifetime.

a natural instinct

A baby's action of smiling is inborn. One might imagine that a baby, watching her mother smiling down at her, does her best to imitate the maternal facial expression. However, it is known from careful observations that this imitation is not necessary. Babies that are, tragically, born deaf and blind also smile when held in a loving embrace by their mothers. What a viewer might find slightly disturbing about these babies' smiles, however, is that they are not directed at the mother's face. This underlines a special quality of the smile that is performed by a baby who can see her mother – it is accompanied by eye-to-eye contact. It is not enough simply for the mouth to smile; for the full impact of this visual signal, a baby's face must also be directed toward her mother and she must stare at her intently as she smiles. The baby does not smile *with* her, but *at* her, and it is this that gives her such a powerful reward.

types of smile

A baby has three types of smile – the reflex smile, the general smile and the specific smile. The reflex smile, or presmile, appears as early as the third day and is seen, on and off, during the first month of life. It is fleeting and barely recognizable as a smile, but is soon detected by eager parental eyes. A common instance of the reflex smile occurs when the baby experiences a neural spasm as she drifts off to sleep while listening to her mother's soothing voice. It may also happen following a sudden influx of energy into her nervous system during a bout of gentle tickling. While the reflex clearly produces a smile on occasions, it is still a muscular reflex and the baby is just as likely to frown from such stimulation at this age.

When a baby is about four weeks old she starts to show a genuine, fully formed greeting smile. Her whole face lights up and her eyes twinkle. She responds in this way to the appearance of an adult face close to hers. This, the general smile, is nonselective – any adult can trigger it. Linked to both experience and expectation, the baby has learned to give the full signal. She has not yet become selective, however, and strangers, as well as parents and familiar family members, receive full-blooded, entrancing smiles. Somewhere around six months all this changes. Now the selective, specific smile appears. The baby no longer smiles at strangers, who may be upset if, a few months earlier, they elicited a broad grin and now find themselves ignored. The baby has learned to distinguish the faces of her loved ones and reserves her greeting smile exclusively for them. The infantile communication system is, at last, personal.

the arrival of speech

A steady development of vocal ability between birth and the age of two years occurs in all children, the world over. Although there is no total consensus of opinion, it is generally agreed that some kind of innate programming is the only possible explanation for the astonishing speed at which a baby learns language. It would appear that his brain is wired for this and it is one of the greatest gifts that evolution has bestowed upon him.

earliest sounds

For the first six months all babies are programmed to start gurgling and babbling in the same way, and it makes no difference whether they are European, African or Asian – they all experiment with the same incoherent sounds. This applies even to deaf children. Parents may think that they are teaching some of these sounds to their tiny babies, but they are not. The babies would make the same sounds, with or without parental involvement, and it is impossible to tell the difference between, for example, the babbling of a Japanese, a Nigerian and a French baby.

tuning in

After the first six months, a new phase is reached and babies become sensitive to the rhythmic qualities of different languages. Research indicates that, by the end of the first year, babies will have tuned in to the particular language spoken at home. In a test carried out in France, adults were played recordings of the preverbal babbling of infants, some of them French and some foreign. Surprisingly, they found it easy to pick out the French babies from the others, even though no single word of French was spoken.

producing sounds

A baby is fully equipped with the complex anatomy necessary to create sounds, but it takes about a year for her anatomy to mature to the point where she can form words in a coherent way. In the earliest months she is only capable of a variety of grunts, cries and babbling sounds.

larynx

At birth, the larynx is about ⅞ inch (2 cm) long and ⅞ inch (2 cm) wide – about one-third of its adult size. The larynx is positioned high up in the neck at this stage, and as the baby grows it slowly descends. Before this descent occurs, the baby's larynx is located immediately below the opening of the oral cavity into the pharynx. This is also the situation found in an adult ape and explains why neither the human newborn nor the adult ape could produce a repertoire of words, even if their nervous systems were wired for it.

vocal cords

At birth, a baby's vocal cords are about ¼ inch (4 mm) in length. These are membranes that fold across the larynx, where they are bombarded by currents of air. Normal breathing, with the muscles of the larynx relaxed, does not produce a strong enough current to make the cords vibrate, so no sound is created. But if the exhalation is sharper and more powerful, and the muscles of the larynx contract to reduce the size of the aperture, then, as the expelled air passes over the cords, it makes the noise that escapes from the mouth: the faster the movement of the air, the louder the sound, and the smaller the gap, the higher the pitch.

At this stage there is no difference between boys and girls. Sex differences only begin to appear in the third year, when the cords of the boy become slightly longer and thicker than those of the girl. At the same time the male larynx becomes slightly longer and larger, but this difference is not marked until the arrival of puberty, when the boy's voice "breaks" and becomes much lower.

tongue and lips

Sounds produced by the passage of air through the larynx and over the vocal cords are rather crude, and it takes a combined action of larynx, tongue and lips to refine them into specific words. The quality of the sounds produced also depends on the cavities of the mouth, nose, sinuses, throat and chest, and it is the exact shape of these cavities that gives each voice its personal quality and resonance.

preverbal sounds

The very first time that the baby exercises her vocal cords, it is to emit a loud cry, following the shock of birth. In the first weeks of life, the cry is about the only sound-signal a baby has to offer, but an alert parent can soon begin to identify different types of crying. These vary according to the particular problem the baby is experiencing (see Crying, page 107). Each cry has a slightly different tonality, pitch and loudness, especially at the beginning, before it develops into full-blooded screaming.

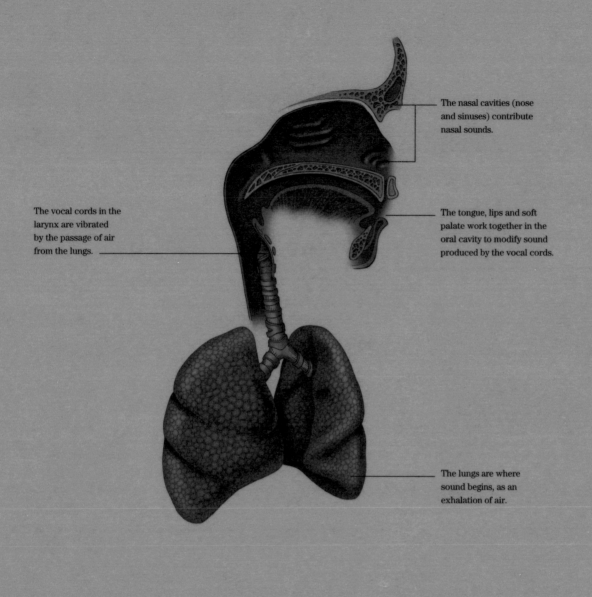

The nasal cavities (nose and sinuses) contribute nasal sounds.

The vocal cords in the larynx are vibrated by the passage of air from the lungs.

The tongue, lips and soft palate work together in the oral cavity to modify sound produced by the vocal cords.

The lungs are where sound begins, as an exhalation of air.

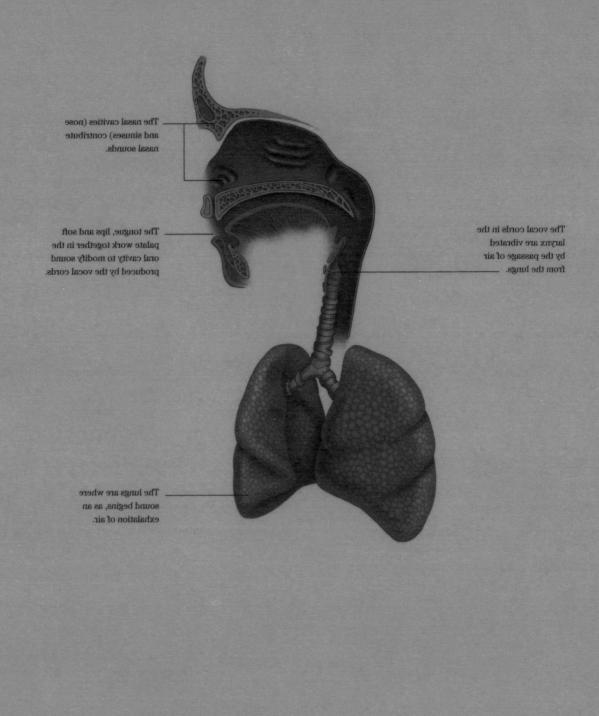

development of speech

While a baby's urge to babble and gurgle in the earliest months is inborn, his later urge to develop this babbling into spoken language is learned by attentive imitation. A baby who instinctively makes single-syllable vowel sounds at the age of three months starts, voluntarily, to make a number of two-syllable sounds at seven months and begins to learn words from eight months. By 10 months, he utters his first word and he has three words by the end of his first year.

vocabulary building

The pace at which a baby's language skills develop is truly astounding. A child that has as many as 19 words by the time he reaches 15 months has some 200 to 300 by the end of his second year and can make rudimentary sentences using verbs, pronouns and plurals. As always, there is considerable variation from infant to infant. For example, one survey of a group of children aged 20 months revealed that a number already had a 350-word vocabulary, while others had learned only six words.

baby talk

Many parents adopt a high-pitched goo-goo kind of baby talk when conversing with their infants. Referred to as "parentese," it involves talking in a sing-song kind of way, typically elongating vowel sounds and making exaggerated facial expressions. Sentences are short and parents tend to talk slowly and deliberately, often repeating a phrase over and over again. All adults do this, throughout the world and regardless of their age or relationship to a baby.

While parentese is beneficial to a young baby, helping him to recognize familiar sounds and words, it is no longer particularly helpful by the time the baby approaches the end of his first year. At this stage the growing infant needs to imitate his parents. If the opposite is happening the learning process is curtailed. Instead, parents who speak to a child in normal adult voices provide the little ones with a much richer, more stimulating variety of sounds and inflections to imitate.

origins of speech

A baby seems to be capable, even in the earliest month of life, of making several different and quite distinct types of "grunt" revealing his mood. One kind of grunt indicates discomfort, for example, another tiredness, another hunger and another gas. It has been pointed out that these grunts, as well as the baby's first attempts to create simple words such as "mama" and "dada," are much the same the world over (see The arrival of speech, page 110). It has therefore been suggested that these utterances, common to all humanity, probably represent the kind of primeval language first used by our ancient ancestors, before humans started splitting into groups and developing different kinds of adult language.

Recordings of baby gurglings reveal that there are four sequences of sound patterns, each consisting of a particular consonant-vowel combination, and that these are common to cultures with adult languages as different as Swedish, Portuguese, Korean, Japanese, French and Dutch. There was probably a time when our evolving ancestors could manage little more than these few utterances. The next step would have been to repeat these primitive sounds in a rhythmic manner – "babababababa" or "gagagagagaga" – to make longer units, and this process is still very common today in the earliest attempts of babies to make words. Learning adult speech is an extremely complex procedure involving the coordination of no fewer than 70 different muscles, and babies have to be patient while slowly gaining full control of these muscles.

listening and babbling

Vocal communication involves two distinct elements – listening to sounds and making them. A baby is always slightly more advanced as a listener than as a sound-maker. She is even able to hear words when she is still inside the womb. This means that she is responsive to parental voices from the day she is born, even though it is several months before she herself starts to make babbling sounds.

babies and listening

When the fetus is six or seven months old, she is already capable of hearing sounds made in the outside world. Tests have shown that a baby's heart rate dips slightly on hearing a new, loud noise. At each repeat of the sound, the baby's reaction lessens until, eventually, there is no observable dip. The baby has become conditioned to that particular sound. If a new sound is now introduced, the dip in heart rate immediately reappears, proving that the fetus can distinguish between one sound and another. Further tests have demonstrated that an unborn fetus is capable of distinguishing between two very similar words and that her listening ability is clearly far in advance of her speaking.

What this demonstrates is that, by the time she is born, a baby has already come to know her mother's voice and can distinguish it from all other voices. Similar experiments with music reveal that a fetus is capable of telling one kind of music from another, and is even able to tell one nursery rhyme from another. There is, of course, no suggestion that she can understand the content of musical compositions or rhymes. What she is detecting is no more than different sound patterns, but even that is extraordinary enough and explains why very young babies are so fascinated by making a variety of simple sounds themselves, as soon as they discover how.

the bubbling phase

The stream of sounds made by a young baby passes through a number of phases during her first year of life, after which it is replaced by the serious business of forming words. When only one or two months old, a baby discovers that she can perform a bubbling action by pushing her tongue out through her slightly parted lips and then closing the lips again. A little bubble of saliva emerges from her mouth. As yet, no sound accompanies this great achievement, but it is the very first step on the long road to verbal fluency. In making this prebabbling action, the baby is mouthing the actions of vocalizing, coordinating her breathing with the movements of the tongue and lips. It is this vital combination that later provides the basis for true speech.

the cooing phase

At the age of three months, audible babbling arrives on the scene. As the weeks pass, this new discovery – the ability to make noises – fascinates a baby more and more, and babbling becomes an obsession. At first there is little more than splutters and grunts and rude noises, but then the first open vowel sounds are made. Now the baby experiments with oooos and aaaas, and parents find it hard not to join in with cooo-cooos and gooo-gooos.

the advanced babbling phase

The babbling reaches a crescendo at the age of six months. It is such fun that a baby often happily burbles away when she is completely alone. Consonants now join the vowels to produce a wide variety of single-syllable sounds. But there is still no relationship between these sounds and any specific object or person. They are "sounds for sound's sake" without any reference or specific meaning – like a singer practicing the scales without making a song.

first words

The first word with specific meaning uttered by an infant is usually "mama" or "dada," and is directed at parents as they chatter to their offspring. It is a moment of great joy, and parents are usually keen to demonstrate the passing of this important threshold to their friends. Unfortunately, when the infant sees an old friend of his father's peering down at him, he is liable to call him "dada" as well.

This is merely a reflection of the fact that, as yet, the infant is only just beginning to put word to person. Mother may also be called "dada," and father "mama," but little by little the links between specific sounds and specific individuals are established. It is this stage that is the true passing of a major threshold.

the preverbal phase

Before words are spoken with a specific meaning, however, there is one final phase of undirected sound-making. This arrives at about seven months and consists of making two-syllable words. Usually the first syllable is the same as the second one, as with "mumum," "dadad" or "booboo." The baby is now exploring, not only more complicated double sounds, but also trying out variations in volume, pitch and speed. He is like a tiny orchestra tuning up before a great concert performance. He cannot play the music yet, but he can at least test out his instruments. His utterances may occasionally sound like true words, but as yet they have no real meaning. The next phase – and the thrill of being able to communicate with his parents – is almost upon him, but not quite. When this stage does finally arrive, it soon sweeps the joys of babbling into the past and replaces them with the more serious business of starting to learn a functional vocabulary.

tone of voice

Vocal communication is more than a verbal exchange. It also involves tonality. A baby is sensitive to two contrasting types of "tone of voice" – smooth and harsh – and he also distinguishes between soft and loud. He dislikes harsh or very loud voices, even when the spoken words are identical to those uttered by smooth, soft voices. If an adult coos "I love you" to a baby, using a warm, gentle, loving tone, he enjoys the words. But if the same adult yells "I love you" using a harsh tone, the baby reacts unhappily. So, as the baby starts to acquire a vocabulary, it is important to remember that each word carries a tonal "modifier" that can dramatically change its significance.

early vocabulary

Once true words with specific meanings are uttered by a baby, it is fascinating to see which ones come first. They are nearly always one- or two-syllable words. Longer words defeat a baby in the earliest phase of speaking. He also ignores short words that relate to anything abstract or intangible. The very first "sentences" usually consist of no more than a noun, and the nouns are always someone or something that is visible at the time. The most popular first words with a meaning are dada, mama, grandma, grandpa, nose, mouth, doggy, kitty, ball, eat and drink, along with the nicknames of brothers, sisters and other family members. As the number of such verbal labels starts to grow, simple verbs are added, creating two-word sentences. As before, the baby's understanding of language is more advanced than his ability to speak it. If the mother asks "Where has kitty gone?", the baby looks around trying to locate the kitten, even though he may not yet be able to say the four-word sentence himself. Baby utterances are always trying to catch up with baby understanding, and it is this race that helps to drive the infant forward to ever better communication skills.

understanding

During the second year of life a toddler makes an incredible transition – she acquires the ability to talk to her parents, to make statements, to ask and answer questions. She effortlessly learns that conversation involves a set sequence of speaking-listening-speaking-listening and she comes to understand the need to take turns.

learning grammar

The simple use of noun and verb in two-syllable sentences can take the toddler a long way. With nouns like "mama" and "dada," "cookie" and "juice," "teddy" and "doggy," and with verbs like "come" and "go," "start" and "stop," "give" and "take," an infant can make a wide range of statements about the immediate present and the world around her. She can also convert her statements into questions by changing the tone. If the statement is "mama gone" there is a lowering of tone with the second word. If "mama gone?" is a question, then the tone of the second word rises.

sentence building

The next stage is to add further words to her conversation. As she approaches her second birthday, a toddler suddenly starts to enlarge her vocabulary and to add extra words to

her old two-word statements. By the age of two, she is probably constructing some three- or four-word sentences. "Mama gone?" might become "Where mama gone?" The toddler refers to herself as "me," as in "me want juice." The two-year-old is now right on the threshold of true conversation. In the year to come, grammar will appear – not because it is painstakingly taught, but because all human beings have an inborn tendency to develop language skills at this age.

the art of deception

One of the verbal skills that a toddler acquires during her second year is the ability to tell a lie – she deliberately sets out to deceive her parents. For example, if the parents are both very busy and a child is feeling bored or neglected she may fake a minor problem or injury to get some attention and perhaps a hug and a kiss. This is not a difficult strategy to understand, even at the tender age of, say, 18 months. What happens is that the infant discovers that if she is distressed, one of her parents will stop what he or she is doing and rush over to her. The sensation of being comforted is stored in her memory and the next time she feels in need of some loving care, it does not require a towering intellect for her to hit on the idea of pretending to be upset or hurt.

New research has revealed that a baby as young as six months may use this strategy to gain attention. Although she cannot talk yet, she is able to control her crying to gain attention. What is so interesting about this calculated action is that it reveals an early understanding on the part of the infant of the relationship she has with her parents. It shows that, from a very tender age, an infant comprehends that her actions have an interactive effect.

word games

The two-year old toddler is an amazing word-learning machine, with his vocabulary growing in leaps and bounds. New words are added and understood every day, but where do they come from? Children's television has been cited as an important source, but in fact this has limited impact. Of greater significance is the back-and-forth exchange of words and sentences with parents, siblings or caregivers. The more time these companions can give to patient conversation, the quicker a toddler becomes fluent in his spoken language.

familiar words

When first learning to grapple with words, a baby responds most strongly to the words he hears most often and thrives on the endless repetition of words. This helps him to learn, day by day, to associate certain words with particular objects or actions. Using a toy such as a teddy bear it is possible to perform little routines day after day – "Teddy sits down. Teddy stands up. Where is Teddy? Teddy is hiding. Teddy is back again." A baby delights in this, and finds his increasing knowledge of what is coming next a pleasant experience.

nursery rhymes

One of the earliest forms of storytelling is the rhyme. Here, it is not important for the toddler to understand all of the words in a rhyme – he usually picks out just one or two. More important is that a rhyme has a verbal rhythm and little actions to perform. Each time the baby hears the rhyme, he eagerly anticipates the accompanying actions and comes to learn that there is a link between these and the words of the song.

reading stories

One of the most delightful of childhood rituals is the telling of bedtime stories. At first, these need to be as repetitive as nursery rhymes. The recognition of a particular phrase in the repeated tale is a moment of joy for the toddler. "Who's been sleeping in my bed?", in the tale of "Goldilocks and the Three Bears," is met with excitement each time the story is told. It is a mistake to think that a bedtime story is "too old" for a particular infant. He may not understand many of the words, but he listens intently nonetheless and, as he does so, gets to know the rhythm and style of the language.

the power of invention

Many parents rely solely on little books of bedtime stories but, as time passes, an even better strategy is to offer the eager learner made-up tales involving his favorite toy. If he loves a toy elephant and insists on cuddling it at bedtime, simple stories about the adventures of this little elephant can emerge night after night. Familiar elements can recur. The elephant is always looking for some water to have a drink and cool down, and this search for water takes him through a series of adventures – a slightly different one each night. Introducing elements of novelty in this way broadens the infant's vocabulary, within a familiar framework. These invented bedtime stories do not need to be great works of literature – the simpler they are the better, and any parent can devise them with the minimum of effort.

how babies learn

intelligence

Intelligence has been defined as the solving of new problems by the combining of past experiences. Therefore, since a new baby has experienced so little of the world, she cannot be said to be intelligent in the strict meaning of the word. She is, however, alert, responsive and eager to learn. Equipped with an amazing brain, complete with ten billion brain cells, she certainly has the potential to become highly intelligent, given enough time.

the learning process

Every day, every week, a baby learns something new and stores the information away in her head. As her body gets stronger, so her brain becomes better programmed, and by the time she is a toddler and is capable of walking around and exploring the world around her, the growing brain has laid the foundations for its future store of knowledge. But there is so much to learn, and it takes many more years before the brain accumulates enough experiences to enable a baby to face the world as an independent adult.

It helps if she has a good start, and an infancy full of rich, varied input is just that. From birth onward a baby has the advantage of a broad range of sensory capacities – hearing, vision, taste, touch, smell, balance and temperature detection. All of these provide her with an increasing range of sensations. She may not yet be at a stage when she can act on these sensations – her slowly developing body may be incapable of carrying out the instructions she would like to give it. This does not mean that her experiences are wasted – merely that she cannot yet react to them. They may not be specific memories that she can rekindle, but are there all the same, deeply embedded in the vast network of cells that make up her young brain.

brain cells

We now know that the brain of a child is much busier than that of an adult. As she grows, her brain cells are like blotting paper, sucking up every scrap of information that seems to have the slightest use. To organize this information her brain cells have to communicate with one another and they do this through connections called synapses. In the brain of the newborn there are about 2,500 synapses attached to each of the ten billion neurons. In the brain of the two-year-old infant, this number rises to 15,000 synapses per neuron, more than we find in the brain of an adult human. The reason that adults have fewer connections is because, as time goes by, many of the connections are lost. The ones used most get stronger and the ones that are little used get weaker and eventually disappear. In the blotting-paper phase of childhood, everything gets sucked up, but later on the brain starts to become selective and to focus on its strengths and eliminate its weaknesses.

importance of environment

Although genetic factors are also very important, for a child to develop a high level of intelligence in later life it seems certain that a rich and varied environment during infancy gives her a huge advantage over a child that spends her first few years in a more sterile world. The more talking, the more music, the more visual excitement, the more social interaction, the more mental stimulation and the more physical activity that an infant experiences, the better are her chances of growing up to be a lively, intelligent, sensitive, responsive adult. And the more playful and exploratory the daily life of an infant is, the more likely she is to grow up to become an imaginative, creative adult.

the brain

If we could look inside a human baby's skull we would see the finest brain on the planet. It has three major regions: the forebrain, midbrain and hindbrain. The forebrain is made up of the cerebrum, thalamus, hypothalamus and limbic system. The most conspicuous part is the cerebrum, with its heavily folded surface called the cerebral cortex. The midbrain is the top inch or so of the brain stem – the pathway for information arriving and leaving the brain. And the hindbrain comprises the cerebellum, the pons and the medulla.

cerebrum

The cerebrum is divided into two convoluted hemispheres. The presence of deep folds and creases makes it possible for the large surface area of the cerebrum to be neatly packed into the small space available inside the skull. The gray outer covering of the cerebrum, the cerebral cortex, is composed of 8,000 million nerve cells, which are held together by 64,000 million glia cells. It is the cerebral cortex that organizes information and tells a baby what he is seeing, hearing, imagining and remembering. Among the folds of the cerebral hemispheres there are some deeper fissures, creating four major, paired lobes.

frontal lobes

The frontal lobes lie directly beneath the forehead. These are the baby's crowning glory. They are the most recent development in the evolution of the human brain and the largest and most complex of all four paired lobes. This is where a baby's intelligence lies, his personality is lodged, his creativity is fostered and all his higher forms of mental activity take place. The frontal lobes also deal with the conscious control of his movements and of his speech.

parietal, occipital and temporal lobes

On top of the baby's brain, just behind the frontal lobes, are the parietal lobes, which deal with sensations of touch, temperature, pressure and pain. They are also concerned with messages coming from inside the body. The occipital lobes that form the region at the back of a baby's brain are primarily concerned with detecting and interpreting visual information. On either side of the brain are the temporal lobes, concerned with such things as hearing, music, fear, the sense of identity and memory.

left and right hemispheres

The left hemisphere of the brain specializes in logical matters. It is concerned with calculations, mathematics and factual information. Analytical thought finds its home here. The right hemisphere is the artistic, creative, imaginative half of the brain, home to intuitive thought. The two are connected by the corpus callosum, a band of thick nerve fibers through which information passes.

thalamus and hypothalamus

The thalamus is a small plum-sized area embedded in the very center of the brain. It acts as a relay station dealing with the transfer of information from the body to the brain and from one part of the brain to another. All sense information, except for smell, is passed through this area of the brain. Below the thalamus is the hypothalamus, a regulator concerned with changing moods and motivation, with sleep, hunger, thirst, heart rate, blood pressure and sexual arousal. It controls the activities of the pituitary gland and the hormonal system (see Glands and hormones, page 42). Around the hypothalamus is the limbic system, a complex part of the brain that controls emotions.

cerebellum

Underneath the cerebrum, toward the back of the brain is the cerebellum – the part of the hindbrain that is concerned with monitoring body posture, balance and movement. During the first two years of life the cerebellum grows very fast so that, by the age of two it is virtually fully grown, unlike the higher centers of the brain. Without this rapid growth the infant would find it difficult to master the art of balancing, walking and running. It is also concerned with controlling respiration and blood circulation.

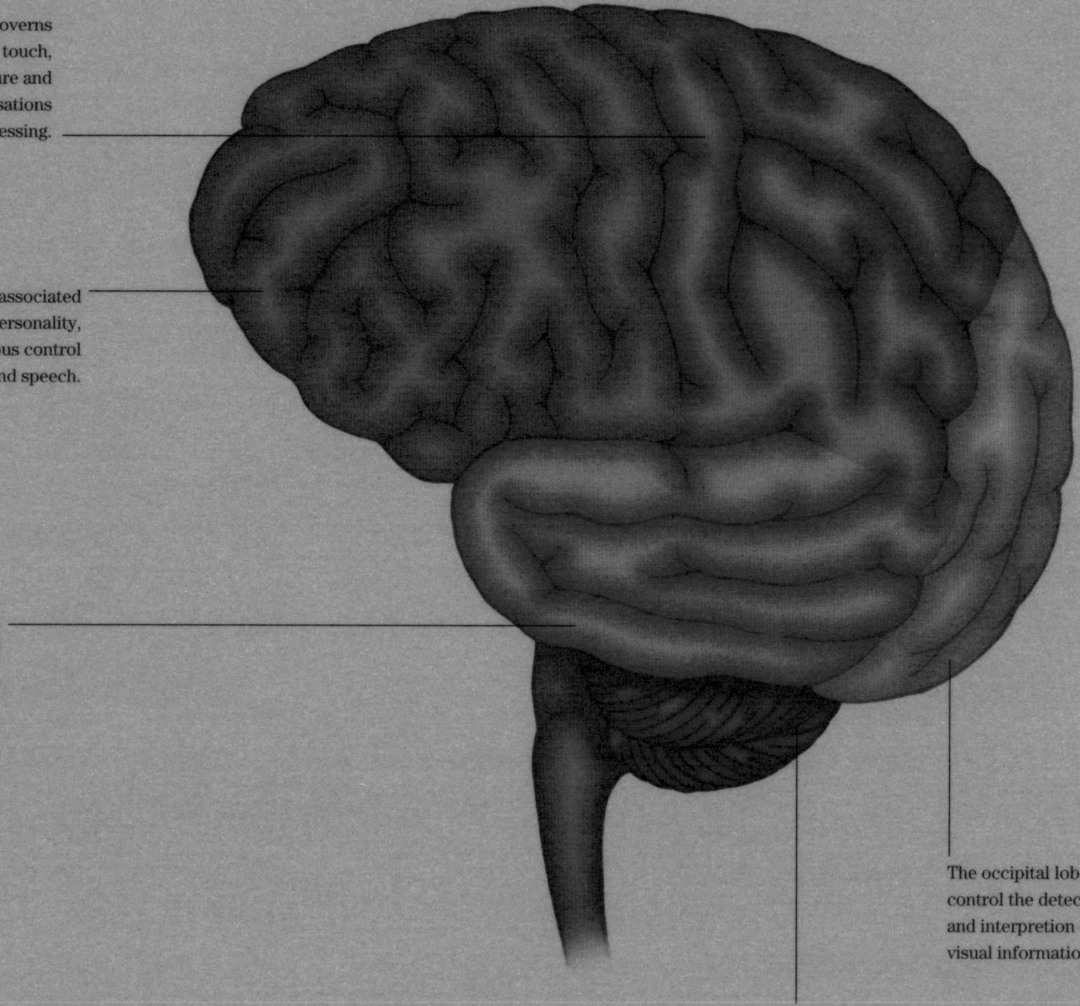

The parietal lobe governs
perceptions of touch,
temperature, pressure and
pain, internal bodily sensations
and visual-spatial processing.

The frontal lobes are associated
with intelligence, personality,
creativity and conscious control
of movement and speech.

The temporal lobes
deal with hearing and
perception of music,
fear, identity and the
storing of memories.

The occipital lobes
control the detection
and interpretion of
visual information.

The cerebellum, part of
the hindbrain, manage
posture, balance and
movement.

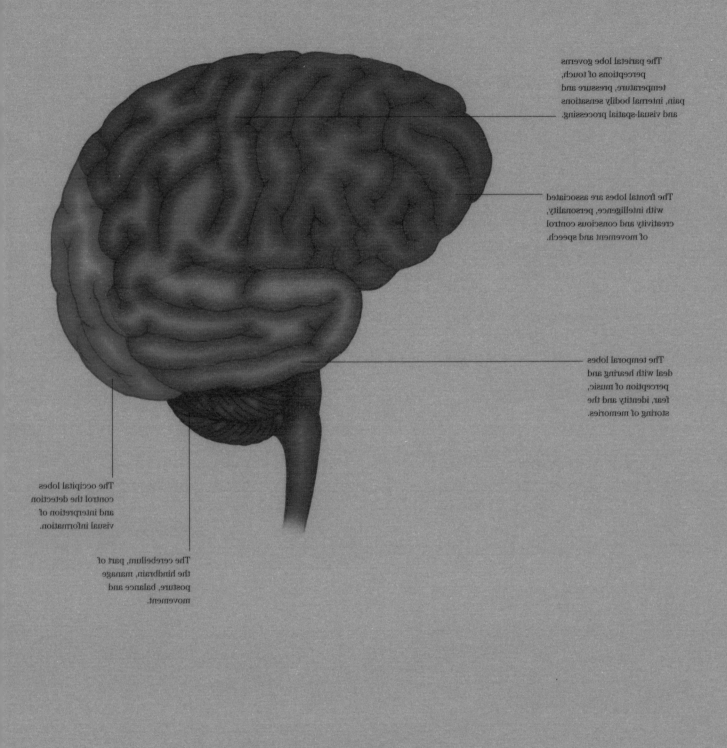

learning environment

What is the ideal learning environment for a young child? What were the first two years of life like for Leonardo da Vinci and Alexander the Great? How did their infantile brains become so successfully programmed that they went on to achieve great things as adults? What do babies and toddlers really need to encourage them to make good use of the amazing brain that nestles inside every human skull?

stimulation

From the earliest days, when lying in her crib staring at the ceiling, a baby is aware of the shapes, colors and sounds around her. Her ears are too sensitive to tolerate very loud or harsh noises, but she seems to enjoy gentle music in a special way, giving her a valuable experience of changing sound rhythms and patterns. Colored shapes floating and moving above her also provide her with an appreciation of fluctuating designs. Being picked up, held, hugged, cuddled and swung through the air all give her sensations of touch and balance.

Later, as a toddler with the great gift of body mobility, she can actively influence the amount of stimulation she achieves. By exploring her world she can put herself into situations in which more and more stimuli are present.

love of the new

Every human baby in the world is born with a craving for novelty or "neophilia" – the love of the new. It is something that is stronger in humans than in any other species. Given a rich, varied and friendly environment, every toddler will spend hours every day trying out new things and exploring different possibilities, as she feeds her growing brain with a variety of sensations and experiences. If she enjoys these activities they become more and more essential to her existence. If she is positively rewarded by her parents for her neophilia, then seeking novelty becomes a basic part of her personality and should last her a lifetime.

fear of the new

Parents have to tread a fine line between protecting a child from danger and allowing her to discover new things. The opposite of neophilia is "neophobia." If a toddler is punished or traumatized as a result of exploring something, she may become what is known as neophobic. This means, literally, having a fear of the new. An unpleasant trauma or accident can have a seriously inhibiting effect on future play and exploration. For example, toddlers often look upon the family dog or cat as a kind of soft toy and may innocently hurt it. If the pet retaliates, such an unexpected attack can create a long-term fear of all cats or dogs.

An experience like this may also stop an infant playing in those specific environments where the incident occurred or even put her off all similar environments or situations. In extreme cases, it may even reduce a child's playfulness in any situation, since she develops a strongly neophobic response to every new stimulus, and this can seriously curtail her learning ability. The learning environment of the child can therefore be negative as well as positive.

playing

Human beings are the most playful animals on the planet. Play is fundamental to our learning as babies and we continue play into and throughout adult life. The only difference here is that we give play different names, such as poetry, literature, music, art, theater, scientific research, athletics and sports. All of these great achievements have their roots in childhood play and it is, therefore, a subject that deserves serious attention.

pattern of play

Put a toddler in a room filled with toys and watch what happens. Before long a clear pattern develops. During play, he focuses on one particular toy and examines it, testing out its possibilities. Then he starts to play with it, hitting it, taking it to pieces, putting it together again, knocking it over, building it up, moving it around from place to place, and so on. After a while, he tires of this toy and moves on to another one, with which he repeats the same experiments. Then he moves on again, working his way around all the toys, one by one. After a while he pauses and then returns to, say, toy number two. This one gets another bout of investigation and play.

play principles

Several play principles are beginning to emerge. The first is the excitement of neophilia, the love of the new (see Learning environment, page 130). A new toy has a special magic that attracts an infant immediately. This is the novelty principle and with human beings it is of crucial importance. It is what fires our curiosity and provokes us to explore new experiences. Ultimately, it is what makes us creative adults.

As the infant finds out what he can do with the toy, he experiments with a variety of actions. This is the play principle of "thematic variation." After he has exhausted all the possibilities of this particular toy, he tires of it and moves on to something else as the urge for novelty reasserts itself.

These play principles apply not just to toys but to all kinds of infant play, including social games such as peekaboo and hide-and-seek, simple athletic actions like jumping, rolling over or falling on to a soft surface, sporting actions like kicking a ball or forms of creative play such as drawing and painting.

play preferences

It is always intriguing to observe which toys or games an infant keeps returning to and which ones he tends to ignore. These early preferences tell us something about a child's future trends and interests. Is he more physical, more musical, more analytical, more fantasy-based, more chaotic, more tidy? Does he prefer taking things apart or putting them together? Are his actions very precise and careful, or more power-driven? And do these various tendencies, once established, last through to the later years and influence adult life?

first play

Babies play before they are able to coordinate their movements, simply attracted by the sound of a rattle, for example, or the bright colors of a mobile (see Early play, page 136). A baby can even play when he is physically passive but mentally active, as in vertigo play, in which he enjoys the thrill of strangely unfamiliar body movements such as being swung high up in the air and then down again. Later, the adventurous toddler may discover the joy of bouncy castles or trampolines, and take the vertiginous thrills to a new level.

exploring objects

As soon as a baby can use his hands to touch and grasp the things around him, he is driven by his innate curiosity to explore his expanding world. Initially he discovers sensations – hot and cold, soft and hard, wet and dry – then gradually, as his experiences accumulate, he learns more about specific objects and how they work. This is all part of a complex learning process that undergoes a number of developmental stages.

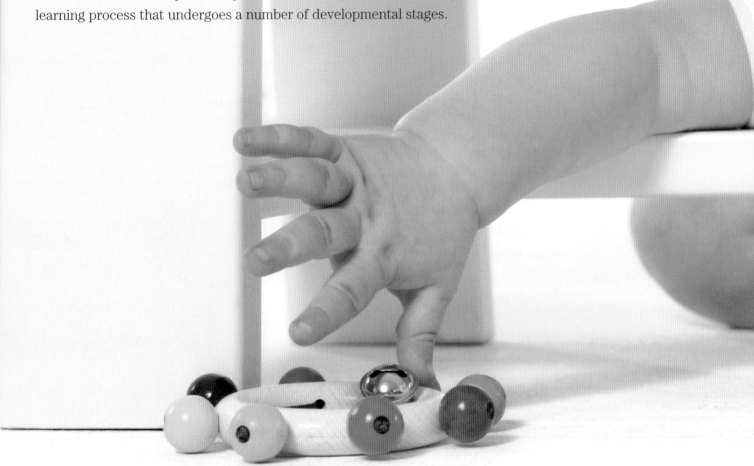

from hand to mouth

Once a baby can coordinate his hand-to-mouth actions, any novel object he is offered is taken up to the mouth for oral investigation. This is because, early on, a baby's mouth is better developed than any other part of the body for feeling sensations, primarily through the action of feeding: it is instinctive for a baby to put an object in his mouth. This "mouthing" phase lasts for a long time and can become a serious hazard in its later stage. A baby's curiosity is such that, once he has learned to crawl, he soon takes off in all directions with remarkable speed, in search of appealing objects to be grabbed and thrust into his mouth. The normal home is full of small objects that can damage a baby in one of three ways. They can be sharper than they appear, like a pair of nail scissors; they can be small enough to be swallowed, like the marbles or toy soldiers of an older child; or they can be chemically harmful, like cleaning liquids and medicines. Even suitable "mouth toys" – plastic objects that can be sucked or chewed – can be dangerous if they have been lying around for too long and gathering dirt.

understanding objects

As well as putting things in his mouth, a baby also shakes, bangs and throws them. From these tests he learns about lightness and heaviness, smoothness and sharpness, and all the other physical properties of the inanimate objects he encounters, discovering how their shape affects the way they move, how one object fits inside another and how they make the different noises when he interacts with them. The knowledge that he gains in this way eventually leads to an understanding of everything from geometry and mathematics to architecture and athletics.

object permanence

One of the most significant developments in a baby's understanding of the objects around him is the discovery of object permanence. First, at around six months, he learns that each object is unique. Before this time, whenever he saw a bird in a tree, he always assumed it was the same bird. Now, he knows that each bird he sees is different.

From here on, the baby gradually begins to understand that an object does not cease to exist when it leaves his sight. The game of peekaboo is a good example of this. A favorite among babies from a very early age, this game involves a parent hiding for a moment and then popping out again. Early on, say at three to six months, the baby learns to expect the parent's head to emerge from behind a door or cushion, but it is not until he is older, six to nine months, that he knows the parent's head is still behind the door, even though he cannot see it. The same is true of a ball that rolls under a sofa and food that drops under the table. This is a fundamental stage of a baby's learning.

early play

A baby loves to play even before she is capable of making coordinated actions. Lying in her crib, she responds with wonder to a hanging mobile catching the light as it floats and twists above her head. If the mobile happens to make a tinkling sound, this adds to its appeal. The baby wiggles her arms and legs around during this visual and audio play, as if she wants to reach up and grab hold of this fascinating new object.

Toys are important in the life of the growing infant because they help to stimulate exploration (see Exploring objects, page 134). The human baby is genetically programmed to have a high level of curiosity and never to stop investigating the world around her. If she is offered only a sparse environment, there is little to encourage this process.

magnified reward

As a child grows stronger she likes to play with toys that give her a sense of power. Every day her muscular control is just a little better than it was the day before, so a toy that gives the impression of achieving more than was expected of it has a special appeal. For example, a solid ball, when hit, moves very little, but a balloon of exactly the same size, when hit with exactly the same force, flies off through the air. The baby performs the same action in each case, but the reaction of the object was much greater with the balloon, so magnifying the reward for the baby's effort.

Any toy that provides a magnified reward in this way gives a baby an appealing sense of power. Another good example is the ball. If a baby throws a wooden building brick across the carpet, it does not move far. If she applies the same effort to a ball, however, it rolls much farther. Any kind of ball has an immediate fascination, therefore. Similarly a toy on wheels moves more easily and is therefore more appealing than a toy that has to be dragged along.

noise and destruction

Hitting toy objects as hard as possible has great appeal, especially for boys. Those toys that make an unusually loud noise when struck are more attractive than those that only make a dull thud. Hitting a drum with a stick, for example, is much more fun that hitting a cushion with the same force. A baby also delights in knocking down a tower of blocks or stacking cups. This is another example of magnifed reward, where a parent takes considerable time and effort to build the tower, yet the lightest touch from the baby brings the whole edifice crashing down. The disproportionately catastrophic result provides the infant with a fleeting sensation of possessing great power.

pick-it-up play

Another early form of play that delights a baby is the pick-it-up routine. A clumsy movement results in some small object falling to the floor. An attentive parent quickly picks up the fallen item and replaces it. The infant pauses for a moment and then knocks it to the floor once more, this time deliberately, as a test to find out if the parent will pick it up again. The parent sees the joke and does so. And down it goes again. A game has begun that has a special appeal – the appeal of the power that the small child has to control her large parent.

complex toys

A toddler often makes his own decisions as to what kind of toy excites him most. Tales abound of the child who is less interested in the expensive train set than in the box in which it came. This is because, unfortunately, many toys are designed with the parent in mind and not the child, so that some of the most elaborate toys also happen to be the least used. There are some exceptions to this general rule, however.

challenge toys

A toy that challenges a child's intelligence can quickly become a favorite, as long as it gives the infant a reasonable chance of success. If the child always solves a problem quickly, or never manages to do so at all, the toy is a failure. But if the child frequently gets it wrong, but sometimes gets it right, he is likely to return to the toy time and time again, drawn by the "occasional reward" factor. For a young baby, piling up blocks to make a tower that eventually falls over (or that he knocks down for fun), is a classic example of a challenging toy. It is not a simple matter of win or lose, but of how many bricks the baby can stack before the tower collapses. More advanced toys of this type appeal as the child grows older.

wheeled toys

One step up from simple building blocks is the four-wheel push-along wagon in which a one-year-old can place the blocks. He puts them in, pushes them to a new place, takes them out, builds them up, puts them back in again, moves to a new location, and so on. This involves standing upright with the support of the wagon handle. While concentrating on pushing, the child inadvertently familiarizes himself with the actions of walking. From here on, mobility increasingly becomes something of an obsession and a baby thrills at exploring the world on ride-along toys such as tricycles and pedal cars.

shape and construction toys

Simple shape-sorters appeal from 12 months, when a toddler readily accepts the challenge of fitting different shapes into holes. The excitement of making a star-shaped brick fit neatly into the star-shaped hole preoccupies him as an enjoyable game while at the same time teaching him a great deal about the geometry of familiar objects. Very simple jigsaw puzzles also offer a challenge, improving a toddler's familiarity with irregular shapes.

Toys made of several pieces that a toddler has to fit together in a certain way to create a whole are more complicated than earlier toys, and introduce the concept of "assembling." They test a toddler's visual awareness as well as hand-eye coordination, which becomes more refined as the months pass and the toddler learns to dress and undress a doll or assemble mechanical devices.

making music

Simple musical instruments that a toddler can hit or press to create a variety of notes also have appeal, the child reveling in the fact that something he does results in a funny noise or tuneful sound. A toddler may be shocked by a jack-in-the-box that springs up toward him after playing a tune, but once he recognizes the shock as a "safe" one (see Humor, page 154), he enjoys the experience again and again.

self-awareness

During her first year, a baby lacks any self-awareness. She is so engrossed in the discoveries she is making about the world around her that she pays little attention to herself. All of this changes during her second year, when she gradually becomes aware of her own identity.

the mirror test

When a tiny baby, just a few months old, is shown her reflection in a mirror it does not seem to occur to her that she is looking at a reflection of herself. She reacts to the mirror as just another toy – an exciting one because, as it moves around, its appearance changes. But she has no idea that she is looking at her own image. A fish or a bird reacts in the same way. If a mirror is placed on the animal's territory, it may attack the image, assuming that it is an intruder. Or, if it is in a mating mood, it may try to make sexual advances toward its own image.

When a toddler reaches the age of about 15 months, a moment of truth arrives. She looks in the mirror, waves her hand and the "other person" waves back in exactly the same way. She tries other actions and each is copied precisely. Eventually the child realizes that what she sees is really herself and not another child. A simple test can prove this, in which an infant is shown her face in a large mirror. She is then taken away and a hat is placed on her head, or a small mark made on her face with some makeup. Seeing her reflection again, she reacts in one of two ways. If she reaches out to touch the hat or the makeup mark on her reflection she has failed the test. If, however, she gazes in the mirror, sums up the situation and then reaches up to touch the real hat on her own head, or the real mark on her own face, she has passed the test, because she has proved that she recognizes the mirror image as her own face. By the age of about 18 months, half of all children tested in this way manage to pass the test. By the age of 24 months this figure rises to three-quarters of all children. And in the third year the remaining 25 percent also pass. To adults this seems such a ridiculously easy test and yet very few animals are capable of passing it. Apart from human toddlers, only chimpanzees, orangutans, dolphins, elephants and just one gorilla have managed it with any certainty.

a growing sense of "self"

This self-discovery and the understanding that she is a separate entity – a small person with her own independent existence – grows stronger as the second birthday approaches and goes a long way to explain the phenomenon known as "the terrible twos" (see A busy age, page 177). At this age, a child, having made the discovery that she is a complete being, like the ones she sees around her, is liable to become rather self-centered and often stubborn. She wants to do things *her* way and may get angry if she is not able to. Controlling her sometimes becomes a battle of wills, and parents need to adopt new strategies to deal with this obstinate phase.

separation anxiety

A toddler has a deep-seated fear of losing touch with his parental protectors. When very young, he may go into a state of screaming panic if he cannot locate his mother or father, or whoever has the role of principal caregiver. As time passes, however, he eventually learns that, in certain specific circumstances like being put to bed, he has to accept the departure of the loved ones, and there is nothing he can do about it. At these moments, he seeks out some form of substitute for the missing caregivers – a "transitional comfort object."

transitional comfort objects

Because the departing mother has a soft, cuddly body, the best substitute for her is something that is soft, smooth and warm to the touch and that the child can press against his cheek and hold tightly in his arms. For many children this means a piece of bedding, such as a blanket, which the child grabs, bunches up and holds to the side of his head. A toddler often falls asleep in this position, with his cheek pressed against the substitute mother's body. This then becomes a favorite object and something for the child to carry around for emergency use whenever he feels a pang of insecurity.

soft toys

A child who has a number of soft toys to play with during the day often selects just one of these as the "special toy" to keep close at all times. It may be a teddy bear, an elephant, a cat or some other character and usually has a very special name. When lost, it can cause panic and even tragedy.

wear and tear

One problem with security objects is that they have to be present, day in and day out, week after week. Eventually the constant hugging and cuddling takes its toll and the favorite blanket or cloth becomes smelly and ragged. At this point the parent decides, for purposes of hygiene, to wash or repair the much loved object. But for the infant, this may remove the special fragrance, or worn texture, that has become an integral part of the experience of cuddling during moments of insecurity. Even worse is the moment when a parent feels that he must go further and replace the original with a new clean one – a change that is often resisted passionately. Transitional objects become so important to their owners that they acquire the character of intimate companions and develop personal identities. So real do they become that, with some individuals, they are retained for years, and in a few cases even into adulthood.

a maternal instinct

With many small girls, anything super-soft or super-cuddly triggers a strangely inverted response in which the child becomes the symbolic parent and the soft toy becomes the symbolic child. The girl cares for her toy with all the tenderness of a mother protecting her child. Although she is giving rather than receiving security, the cuddling involved still operates successfully as a destressing device.

gender and the brain

How alike are the brains of boys and girls at birth? Does the way in which they are built, or function, result in specific gender characteristics from day one of life outside the womb? Recent investigations suggest that this certainly is the case and, moreover, that such developments begin even earlier, about halfway through pregnancy.

the brain in the womb

When, at about five months old, the testicles of a male fetus start to produce testosterone, there is a significant hormonal impact on the developing tissues of the brain. Enzymes work on the male sex hormones so that they bind with the brain tissue and begin an irreversible transformation. The result of this is that, even as early as the 26th week of pregnancy, it is possible to distinguish a male fetal brain from a female one, and that some of the differences between them are visible to the naked eye.

brain scans

Following substantial new research, brain scans have revealed, for example, that male babies have more asymmetrical brain hemispheres than female babies. They also have more white matter and less gray matter, when compared with female babies. Also, females have more gray matter in the newer parts of the cerebral cortex, while male babies have proportionately more gray matter in the older, more primitive parts of the brain.

Another interesting difference is that, with female brains, there is a greater symmetry in what is called the "higher association cortex." This is the part of the brain most concerned with complex mental processes. Male brains are significantly larger on the left. What little asymmetry there is in female brains reveals that their association cortex is slightly larger on the right. Bearing in mind that the left hemisphere is predominantly concerned with analytical thought, while the right brain is more involved with intuitive thinking, it would seem that perhaps the old wives' tale about the importance of "women's intuition" has, after all, a serious basis in fact.

implications for the future

These early differences in the brains of male and female babies are long lasting and brain-scan tests carried out on adult males and females reveal that they have a long-term impact. During these tests it is possible to see which parts of the brain "light up" (that is to say, become active) when problems are being solved. Females, for example, use both hemispheres at the same time when processing verbal information. Men use only the left hemisphere. When posed with a navigational problem, such as how to reach a particular address, women used mostly the right side of their cerebral cortex, while men employed the left hippocampus. With emotional responses, females mostly use their cerebral cortex. With men, emotional activity is stuck in an older part of the brain – the amygdala. Research has shown that a testosterone surge in infancy appears to enlarge the amygdala, making it visibly bigger in boys' brains. By adulthood, the male amygdala is 16 percent larger than the female's.

If some of these anatomical details are confusing, all one needs to remember is that, from birth and even from before birth, the male and female brains differ in structure, organization and operation. However, although these differences mean that males and females have different thought processes, it does not mean that evolution forces them to act differently, only that they arrive at their conclusions – often perhaps the same conclusions – in different ways. As one brain specialist put it: "The differences in what women and men can do is small; the difference in how they do it is large."

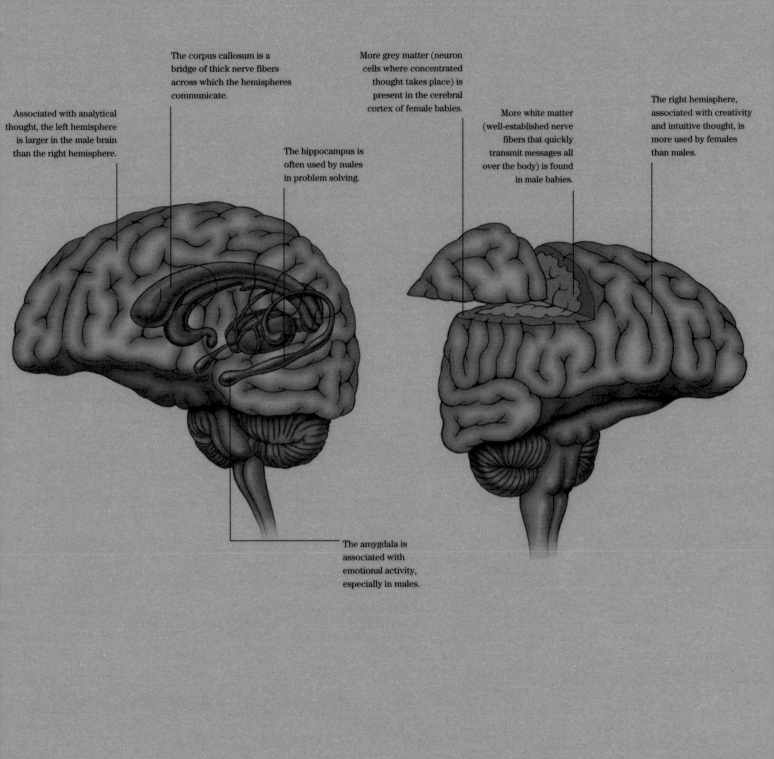

Associated with analytical thought, the left hemisphere is larger in the male brain than the right hemisphere.

The corpus callosum is a bridge of thick nerve fibers across which the hemispheres communicate.

More grey matter (neuron cells where concentrated thought takes place) is present in the cerebral cortex of female babies.

More white matter (well-established nerve fibers that quickly transmit messages all over the body) is found in male babies.

The right hemisphere, associated with creativity and intuitive thought, is more used by females than males.

The hippocampus is often used by males in problem solving.

The amygdala is associated with emotional activity, especially in males.

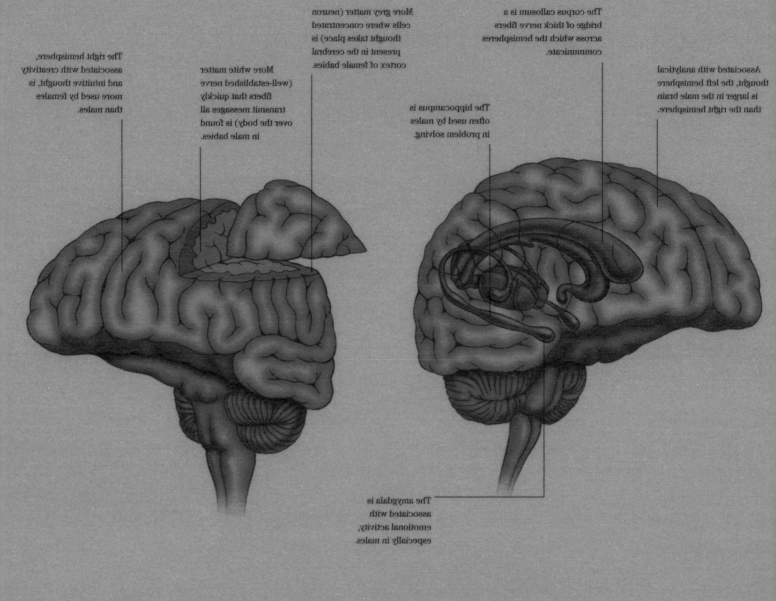

emotional life

personality

Parents with more than one child marvel at how much they differ in personality, even from a very early age. One baby may be quiet, another alert, another active and another screaming, with different personalities developing despite a child receiving the same loving treatment as his siblings. Assuming they are healthy babies, what causes these early differences?

in the genes

Although we still know very little about how the genes influence human personality, it seems certain that environmental differences cannot explain all the variations in character that we see among brothers and sisters. For some, the idea that genes can control something as subtle and complex as an individual human personality seems far-fetched, but this overlooks the long-term impact of certain very simple differences in character.

personality types

Take the quality of playfulness. The main evolutionary trend of our species has been to make us all increasingly playful, and to make this playfulness last longer and longer, right into adult life. It is this quality that has made us so inquisitive, exploratory and inventive. And it is our intense curiosity that has made us successful as a species. Through evolution our playfulness has been genetically enhanced, but this new development is rather uneven. Some of us are more inquisitive than others and this difference can be seen at a very early age. Some toddlers are novelty-seeking extroverts, while others are harm-avoiding introverts, and there is a whole range of intermediates in between.

Supposing a single genetic influence determines a baby's novelty-seeking (neophilic) urge, and that another gene influences the baby's novelty-avoidance (neophobic) urge (see Learning environment, page 130). The balance between these two genetic influences in any one baby places him somewhere on the extrovert/introvert scale. Given this genetic starting point, a baby's environment will do the rest. If a novelty-seeking baby grows into a toddler who is permitted and encouraged to strengthen this quality, a highly nonconformist, inventive adult is in the making. If a novelty-avoidance baby becomes a toddler who is never

encouraged to explore and may be punished for doing so, then a conformist, unimaginative adult is in the making. The first avoids routine and demands new experiences, while the latter is content to accept the status quo.

There are many other variations. What happens if the playfully inquisitive toddler is punished for being so outgoing? Or if the placid harm-avoider is encouraged to take risks and seek new sensations? Each of these combinations, with genetics and environment pulling in different directions, results in different kinds of personality. In addition, there are all the intermediate states, giving a huge range of possible personality variants, simply from the influence of one basic genetic factor.

parental influence

Parents influence these personality developments, even if they do not mean to do so. If a toddler seems too placid and is uninterested in novelty, a parent may spend more time trying to build up a basic level of excitement in the child. If done gently, this helps to create a more balanced adult. If done too forcefully, it may create a stressed and anxious individual. Alternatively, if a toddler is hyperactive and intensely inquisitive about everything in his life, a parent may start to worry about the possibility of risks and dangers. So, this parent may try to introduce calming measures. Again, done gently, this may help a toddler to avoid serious risks without cramping his style. But if it is taken too far, and the toddler is repeatedly restrained from his playful investigations, a seriously frustrated personality could result.

One thing seems certain: within the first few years of life, most children lay down the personality type that accompanies them through their adult life and into old age.

baby moods

What influences a baby's moods, so that one moment she is gurgling happily and the next she is fractious and miserable? Observations of babies reveal that they are happiest in an atmosphere of gentle stimulation. They become bored and restless if there is no activity of any kind and they become anxious if they are surrounded by intense activity. But if gentle stimulation suits them best, what kind of stimulation should this be?

life in the womb

Before she is born, a baby is exposed to certain sounds and movements that she later associates with perfect peace and security. The dominant sound she hears is the rhythmic beat of her mother's nearby heart. And the dominant movement is the equally rhythmic swing of her mother's abdomen as she walks. If these two sensations become deeply embedded in the developing brain of the fetus, it is possible that they come to spell safety and protection even after the child has been born. How can this be tested?

the mother's heartbeat

When she is relaxed, a pregnant mother's heart beats about 72 times per minute. In a series of tests, observations were made on how long it took babies to fall asleep when their bedrooms were silent. They were then put to bed on different occasions to recordings of a human heart, with very slow, very rapid and rather irregular heartbeats. Finally, recordings of gentle lullabies were played to them. On each occasion careful note was made of the time it took the little ones to fall asleep. The results were striking.

Babies that could hear the regular heartbeat sound at 72 beats per minute fell asleep twice as quickly. Everything else – silence, lullabies and irregular, fast or slow heartbeats – failed to calm the infants. Even a metronome clicking away at the correct speed did not satisfy them. Clearly the mother's heartbeat was deeply imprinted as a mood-changing stimulus during the later months in the womb. Such observations explain why a mother favors her left arm when holding a baby close to her chest. Without realizing it she places the baby's ear close to her heart and in this way helps to keep her mood calm. This has nothing to do with a mother being right-handed: 78 percent of left-handed mothers also prefer to cradle their babies in their left arms. What is more, a study of 466 "Madonna and child" paintings dating back over several hundred years, show the same bias. In 373 of them (80 percent) the child is depicted cradled in the Madonna's left arm. Incidentally, observations of women carrying parcels when out shopping reveal that there is no left bias in this instance – 50 percent carry the parcel on their left, while 50 percent do so on their right.

the mother's walking movement

A fetus senses the slow, rhythmic walking pace of her pregnant mother and this, too, can act as a mood-calming influence. Many a mother, trying to get her infant off to sleep, intuitively starts pacing up and down with the baby in her arms. The embrace, combined with these smooth movements, rekindles the experience of life in the womb and hastens a calm mood that quickly leads to sleep.

kangaroo care

A premature baby is usually kept in an incubator where she has no contact with her mother's body, and therefore no exposure to the maternal heartbeat. In one hospital in San Francisco, experiments were carried out in which the tiny premature babies were brought out of their incubators and placed on their mothers' chests for a while each day. Those that received this "kangaroo care" developed so much faster than the others that they were able to leave the hospital in half the time. If any test underlines the extraordinary power of the maternal heartbeat as a baby-calmer, this is it.

emotional intelligence

Emotional intelligence is a measure of our ability to control our own emotions, understand the emotions of others and to deal with social relations in a helpful way. It is the kind of intelligence that makes for a good negotiator, a compassionate friend or a kind colleague. An individual who has high emotional intelligence is a cheerful, calming influence in a group. Babies and toddlers have not yet reached a stage where emotional intelligence is highly developed, but the behavior of their parents toward them can help to build the foundations of future skills in this area.

learning from parents

As a baby grows, he learns about the world in two ways. He learns about the physical world by testing objects, playing with toys and experimenting with the movements of his own body (see Exploring objects, page 134). But no matter how high his IQ becomes, it says nothing about his social skills. These he must learn from his parents. During the first two years of life, his parents or primary caregivers are his major source for discoveries about how people interact with one another. If he is lucky enough to be a much-loved infant, he has a higher chance of becoming a loving adult. All he has to do is to achieve the great emotional switch from "receiving love" to "giving love."

learning about other living things

It is difficult for a baby to grasp the difference between an inanimate object and a living being. He is likely to make little distinction between a soft toy and a live kitten. It has to be said that infants are not usually very good with pets. A baby may hit a kitten simply because he doesn't understand what he is doing. To him it is just another test, like banging a drum or throwing a toy out of a crib. This is where parents can, with great patience, start the long process of training him in handling relationships. The key moment of understanding comes when he becomes aware that the kitten feels pain when hurt, just like he does. When he realizes that other living beings have the same feelings as himself, his emotional intelligence is born. To get this across when the infant is younger than two years old is not easy, but with care it can be done. The sooner this process begins, the more deeply it becomes embedded in the brain.

bad parents, good parents

Toddlers who are treated badly by their parents and given the minimum of loving attention, are slow to learn social skills and may never fully develop the ability to sympathize with others or care about their pain. As adults they may remain permanently weak in this respect. Individuals who grow up with low emotional intelligence usually have poor self-control and are often in need of anger management.

Toddlers who are lucky enough to grow up in a happy, loving household absorb the kind of interactions they observe taking place around them. Parents or siblings who are always cheerful, helpful and full of laughter influence the emotional learning of an infant even when he is not directly involved. He sees what is going on and stores away his experiences of how people treat one another. If he sees kind acts performed by one adult toward another, he absorbs the concept of kindliness more easily than if such observations are rare.

striking a balance

It is true that all human beings are born with both competitive and cooperative urges built into their brains, but the balance between these two impulses is easily disturbed. A toddler that sees too much conflict may begin to think of this as the social norm. A toddler who sees nothing but loving actions may grow up unprepared for the harshness of adult life. A toddler who experiences a lot of love and occasional discipline stands the best chance of being the best equipped to face the adult world when he grows up – with a well-developed emotional intelligence.

humor

Having a sense of humor is a major advantage for any adult. Laughter releases endorphins into the bloodstream that act as natural painkillers. Also, tests have shown that a bout of laughter lowers blood pressure, boosts the immune system that fights diseases and reduces the level of stress hormones.

first laugh

For a baby with playful parents, laughter starts some time in the fourth or fifth month. They do something to give the baby pleasure and the baby smiles. They repeat the action and the baby smiles again. If they do it again, a little more strongly, the smile turns into a happy, gurgling sound. Little more than a gutteral noise at this stage, this is nevertheless true laughter as opposed to a simple reflex reaction to a stimulus (see Smiling, page 108). Actions most likely to elicit a baby's first laugh include a "boo!" sound made by a smiling father or a "raspberry" noise as he blows gently against his baby's chest. A baby also responds with laughter to bouncing up and down on an adult's lap, or when the father hides his face with his hands and then quickly lowers them. Other actions that may produce the first laugh include pretending to drop a baby and then quickly halting her fall, lifting her high in the air and swinging her from side to side, or gently tickling her.

What characterizes all of these actions is the mild element of shock, pitched at exactly the right level. A baby laughs because she experiences what we might call a "safe shock." The loud "boo!" frightens her but she knows that it is her protector, the trusted father, who is making the sound, so she reads the shock as safe. And this is precisely what adults do when they laugh at a joke. Nearly all jokes are shocking, but because a joke is delivered by a comedian or by someone who is clearly not hostile toward his audience, people laugh instead of getting angry or frightened.

the structure of a laugh

A baby's soft gurgling laugh gradually develops into the loud, almost shouted laugh of the toddler. These laughs are a series of short, rhythmically repeated exhalations, sounds represented in print as "ha ha ha." If any one of these "ha" sounds were extended in length it would become a cry for help or a wail of pain. But before this can happen, it is cut short and the brief, staccato "ha" is repeated. It is as if the baby, responding to the shock of her father's action, starts to cry out in alarm, but then checks herself almost immediately when she realizes that the shock is a safe one.

funny games

Relief at learning that this type of shock does her no harm makes her want to do it all over again. Before long she learns that she, too, can make others smile and laugh by manipulating her actions, vocalizations and body language. This reinforces her sense of fun and develops her social skills enormously. From now on the baby wants to engage in as many funny games as possible.

fears

While the fear of an adult may be irrational, the fear of a baby often makes very good sense. Because a baby has complete trust in his protective parents, it is inevitable that, if he senses a loss of this protection, he will panic and start crying. This sounds the alarm and helps to increase the chances of rescue. In addition, infants are sensitive to exposure to unusually strong or sudden stimuli that disturb the peace and quiet of their preferred world.

fear of noise

Passengers flying in jetliners with very small babies notice that bouts of uncontrollable screaming often accompany takeoff and landing. This is because a baby's delicate ears hurt, both from the sudden roar of the engines and from the pressure on his eardrums with the rapid change in altitude. His ears are highly sensitive and any loud noise distresses him.

fear of falling

Another fear is that of falling. A baby reacts with panic to any dramatic, unexpected shift in his position. The tense and jerky movements of a nervous or agitated mother act as a signal to her newborn baby that there is danger about. Should the mother pass her newborn to her own mother, who then holds him gently and peacefully, he suddenly feels safe again and relaxes. Smooth, slow, gentle actions calm every baby.

fear of strangers

Up to the age of about six months, a baby does not distinguish between close relatives and strangers and is quite happy for either to pick him up. From six months of age, however, he starts to recognize his nearest and dearest and identifies them as individuals. Should a stranger try to pick him up now, he may panic and start screaming. This is particularly distressing for those relatives who visit only occasionally – an aunt or grandma, for example – and who may not understand why a baby, who loved being held a month ago, has suddenly turned against her. What has she done? The answer is that she has not been around every day, to become one of the baby's "familiars." She is now classed as a stranger and viewed as potentially dangerous. Eventually the infant learns that even strangers can be friendly and can be trusted, but this takes time and cannot be hurried.

fear of getting lost

When a baby becomes a mobile toddler he loves to explore, but he always tries to keep one eye on his parents. If his explorations suddenly take him out of sight of his protectors, there is a moment of panic and he rushes back toward them. If he gets lost in a crowd, the panic he suffers becomes desperate and he is difficult to pacify until reunited with a lost parent, to be cuddled and hugged until the sobbing subsides. He has, in fact, suffered from a double fear, that of separation anxiety and also that of stranger anxiety in coming into contact with any of a number of people who helped him try to find his parents.

fear of the dark

If a baby cries when left alone in his crib and the nursery light is turned out, the chances are that he is not frightened of the dark, but of the separation from his protector. Giving the baby a nightlight does not solve this problem, therefore. It is unnatural for a baby to be left alone by his parents and intense crying should make them realize this. It is not until a child is about two years old that his imagination starts to create lurking monsters at the foot of his bed in his darkened bedroom. This is a natural phase and most small children go through it, sometimes in an extreme form, accompanied by scary nightmares and bad dreams.

phobias

Fears and phobias are two different things. Fears are useful responses to something that can cause harm. Phobias are irrationally powerful responses to something that offers little or no threat. Technically, phobias are referred to as "anxiety disorders." They do not usually develop until a child is about four years old, but their roots may lie deeper, in the world of the two-year-old. For some unknown reason, phobias are twice as common in females as in males.

origins of phobias

If a two-year-old is involved in a traumatic event, such as accidentally locking herself in a closet when playing hide-and-seek, her brain may store away this painful experience and retain a deeply embedded association between small spaces and panic. Later in life, this same individual may find herself in a small crowded room and suddenly experience an irrational state of blind panic.

Because the original moments of panic that result in later phobias occur so early in life they are usually difficult to recall by conscious effort. Instead they are stored away in the unconscious mind and hidden from view. An adult who has a panic attack may have no idea why a particular activity, event or object causes such uncontrollable horror. Only a period of deep psychoanalysis may unearth the true childhood cause.

A survey of the most common phobias gives some clues as to their possible origins. Top phobias include: being confined in enclosed spaces, being faced with open expanses, being present in a large crowd, scaling heights, sinking in water, speaking in public, flying and contact with certain animals such as dogs. Looking at this list, it is easy to see how a two-year-old could have bad experiences with most of them – experiences that become deeply suppressed but remain stubbornly present.

preventing phobias

During her energetic, exploring phase, a two-year-old is always going to be at risk, no matter how many precautions a concerned parent may take. An inquisitive child may climb up high somewhere and then find that she cannot get down again. Waiting desperately for rescue in a state of panic could easily leave its mark on the juvenile brain, but there is no way that a parent can eliminate all climbing possibilities from the environment of the child. The same is true of water, getting lost or an encounter with a dog.

leading by example

If a trauma does occur, it then becomes important to react to it in an appropriate manner. If a parent also shows undue alarm, a child's brain automatically registers the experience as something that was not only unpleasant, but that "was so awful it even panicked my protector." Without the parental panic, the child may simply register "falling in water" or "climbing too high" as something to fear and to avoid sensibly in future. With the parental panic, the experience may become so intense that it develops into a full-blown phobia of water or heights that may last a lifetime.

feelings of security

A toddler's powerful urge to explore has to be balanced by a need to feel secure. Running around in open spaces and investigating distant objects may be attractively exciting but it can also be slightly scary: it takes a toddler too far from his home base, his protectors and his safe retreats. The ideal solution is for the toddler to explore while maintaining contact with something that makes him feel secure.

attachment to parents

Nothing makes an infant feel more secure than close contact with his parents. He can enjoy this security while exploring by walking hand in hand or by running off, keeping an eye on his parents' movements and running back to them every so often for an exchange of words, a hug or a cuddle.

dens and cubbyholes

A toddler at the crawling stage often develops a passion for entering closets and then popping out again. It is not so much that he is playing a hiding game, as that he is looking for a little "home" in which he feels secure and protected against the dangers of the outside world. Some parents erect a small tent on the lawn in the yard. A toddler enjoys using this as a miniature home from which he emerges from time to time to explore the outside world, but returns to it as a reassuring, safe base. Other parents buy a toy house for indoors that is just big enough for a toddler to creep inside. Large cardboard boxes serve the same end. These small, semi-enclosed spaces seem to trigger off a primeval need to occupy a little den – a tiny dwelling – or, for those seeking a more Freudian interpretation, to return to the womb.

collecting and hoarders

Once he has a special place in which he feels safe from the world, a toddler may start to embellish it with collected objects. He seeks out small toys and carries them back to the inside of his den, where he uses them to improve the atmosphere of this secure, customized space. This is the first sign of a toddler's interest in "personal possessions." At this stage, the possessions are rarely of any lasting interest. When he abandons the den in favor of some new activity,

he often ignores his trophies, leaving them behind for his parents to tidy up. For some individuals this collecting urge soon wanes, while for others it gets stronger and stronger until, as adults, they become addicted to decorating their houses with collected possessions that make them feel more "at home" and therefore more secure. It is almost as if modern collectors are re-enacting, in a symbolic way, the behavior of their ancient hunter-gatherer ancestors, whose whole lives were dominated by the idea of bringing animal and plant foods back to the small settlement where the tribe felt as safe as it could from the hazards of life.

defiance

A toddler's emotional life changes as she approaches her second birthday. She is likely to be more confident and outgoing now, and expects her wishes to be paramount. One way in which she expresses her willfulness and growing independence is through defiance. Parents are sometimes surprised at how suddenly their erstwhile compliant child can enter this new phase of development.

the power of refusal

A toddler discovers that uttering the word "No!" has a fascinating impact. It provokes a powerful reaction in the parent and a dramatic, if brief, encounter follows in which the battle of wills is, for the infant, its own reward. It is a new kind of interaction – an emotional novelty – and the infant loves to play with it, testing the parent to see how far she can push the boundaries. Unfortunately, once the child has started to play this refusal game, she does not know how to stop, and eventually there may be a showdown that can be stressful for both parties.

outwitting a defiant toddler

Toddlers are notoriously stubborn but may respond more positively to a number of avoidance tricks that parents play. One solution is the "two choice" gambit. Instead of making a simple request, a parent offers a couple of alternatives. Instead of saying "Drink your milk," the instruction becomes a question, such as "Would you like milk or orange juice?" The response "Neither" has probably not arrived on the scene yet, and the happy result is therefore a choice of one drink or the other.

The second strategy is the "countdown" gambit whereby the child has to make up her mind about something before her parent finishes counting down from ten to one. Surprisingly, this usually works because it becomes a game that is fun to play, and replaces the novelty of saying "No."

The third strategy is a verbal solution. A toddler who shouts "No!" may, in reality, simply be imitating a parent, as she does in many other ways, so it is always worth exploring alternative means of negative expression. The two-year-old may know "yes" and "no," but probably does not know many nuances, such as "maybe," "perhaps," "soon" or "later." Explaining these words gives the child an interesting challenge in which she uses these less negative terms to flex her muscles, simply to show that she understands them.

learning to differentiate

There are times when the situation is so serious that all games are off. If a toddler is about to do something dangerous an emphatic "No!" from the parent is appropriate and must be obeyed. It sometimes helps if there is a key word tagged on after "No!" – a word that has been discussed before, in a quiet moment. A parent can shout "Serious!" immediately after "No!", for example, if it is carefully restricted to emergencies and is never used at other times. The toddler registers this as a "special circumstance" and reacts accordingly.

toddler tantrums

The accomplished toddler is buoyant and outgoing. He is now a walking, talking bundle of energy and the world is his oyster. He is the center of his universe and he soon starts making demands, some of which cannot be met. There are moments when a little discipline is necessary and the dreaded "No!" has to be uttered.

the full-blast temper tantrum

The first time a toddler is inhibited in this way, he may completely lose control, screaming, shouting, crying, kicking, throwing, hitting, writhing, flailing his arms and legs and sometimes holding his breath dramatically (see Crying, page 107). Such an outburst usually lasts between 30 seconds and two minutes, the intensity being such that it quickly burns itself out. Any anger expressed by the parent only makes matters worse and attempts actively to calm the child usually fail also.

There is nothing abnormal about these explosions. Even adults occasionally lose their tempers, curse and swear, and storm out of a room slamming the door. We may have learned to control ourselves enough not to do this very often and, when we do explode, we stop short of screaming and writhing around on the floor, but the two-year-old has yet to develop this degree of self-control. For him, the intense frustration he feels drives him to perform the most exaggerated forms of protest his little body can muster, and this is what makes it so frightening to watch.

Although two years is the peak age for temper tantrums, they can occur as early as one year or as late as four. As many as 80 percent of children in this age group have them at some point and they are just as common in girls as in boys. Some children are particularly prone to them during this period of their lives and, for a while, tantrums may even become a daily event. Others, typically those with an unusually placid, good-natured personality, hardly ever display tantrums and, if they do, they are rather minor affairs, with little more than a whining, crying interruption in what they are doing.

what causes tantrums?

A toddler's failure to get his own way can cause a tantrum. For example, if he wants to do something that his mother is doing, and she stops him because she knows it is beyond his ability, the frustration of his desire for self-expression and independent action easily leads to him losing control.

The same is true when a toddler fails to make something work or is unable to achieve a goal he sets himself. He is at an age where he can envisage the successful completion of a task he embarks upon, but his body may not yet be capable of achieving it. In other words, he can understand what he must do before he can actually do it physically. If, after trying and trying again, he repeatedly fails, he may eventually explode, destroying the object of his frustration. It may be a hard lesson, but he is learning his limitations, and it is a valuable experience for him. Little by little he comes to appreciate his mental abilities, his physical powers and his social influences, and also discovers where their boundaries lie.

gender differences

From birth, male and female babies show a number of inborn gender differences, the origins of which lie in prehistoric times. When our ancient ancestors took up hunting and gathering as a way of life, the females were too valuable to risk on the hunt, which then increasingly became the preserve of the males. The females did almost everything else and were at the center of tribal society, while the males went off looking for meat.

the hunting male

As they became more and more specialized as hunters, the males developed stronger, larger and more muscular bodies: this is reflected in the sizes of male and female babies at birth, the average male baby weighing ½ pound (225 g) more than the average female. Hunters had to be quiet when pursuing prey, more stoical and less emotional: this is reflected in the fact that male infants cry less than females. Males also had to be prepared to take risks and male toddlers are generally more adventurous than females. Males had to become good trackers, chasers and aimers when engaged in hunting, and male babies seem to be better than females with spatial awareness, developing throwing skills and ball play. Male hunters had to fashion efficient weapons and male babies seem to enjoy hitting and banging toys more than female babies do.

the multi-tasking female

The prehistoric females, left to rear the young and organize society in the frequent absence of the hunting males, evolved as naturally more cautious, more caring and more efficient at doing several things at once. Instead of the single-minded personality of the male hunter, the female developed greater multi-tasking abilities and a more patient, cooperative personality. Female sense organs of taste, smell and hearing became better developed than those of the male and, being more vital to the tribe's reproductive success, the females also evolved better resistance to illness and to periods of starvation. As tribal organizers, their verbal skills and vocal fluency were better than those of the males. They became better communicators. Most of these differences can be seen among male and female toddlers, where boys are already generally more taciturn than girls and less concerned with organizing their play activities.

language differences

During the second year of life, when toddlers are starting to speak, certain other verbal differences begin to appear between boys and girls. Girls tend to start using words that describe emotions more often and earlier than boys do. "Like" and "dislike," "love" and "hate," "sad" and "happy," are terms that spring more easily to female lips during the very early stages of language acquisition, probably reflecting the fact that already, at this tender age, girls are more concerned with fluctuating emotional states, while boys are trying to suppress their emotional feelings.

Other language differences that appear very early are the superior fluency of girls and their greater use of discussion with one another to solve problems. Girls also like to use more nouns than boys and are keener on giving things names. Boys are more interested in talking about actions. It is difficult to tell for certain how much these verbal differences owe to inborn characteristics of the male and female infants and how much is down to parental influence. Both are at work and it is hard to separate them. It is certainly true that parents talk differently to male and female toddlers, but just how much this owes to different feedback from their children and how much to their own preconceived ideas about masculinity and femininity is hard to say.

babies and their siblings

When a baby is born he finds himself in a world already occupied by other people. If he is the child of a single mother, living alone in a city apartment, he may find himself in a very small community made up of just himself and his solitary parent. At the other end of the scale, he may find himself in the middle of a huge extended family comprising mother, father, several older children, an aunt and uncle, some grandparents and some close friends.

In tribal societies he becomes just another addition to the village or settlement, with the mother gaining support from almost everyone around. In modern times, the extended family has gone into a rapid decline, with family groups getting smaller and smaller, and relatives becoming more and more remote. For the new baby these social changes can have a dramatic impact.

the only child

A child without any siblings has both advantages and disadvantages. The advantages are that he enjoys the undivided attention of his parents and other caregivers. He has everything to himself. There are no brothers or sisters with whom he must share his toys. The home space is all his. There are no squabbles. He is the king of his castle. The disadvantages are that life will not always be like this and he is not able to learn the hurly-burly, give-and-take of social existence at an early age. By the time he starts going to preschool he already has a clear concept of himself as the center of attention, and he faces a much steeper learning curve than other toddlers who grow up surrounded by competing siblings.

It is not his fault that he has become self-centered: he had nobody else of his own generation on whom to center his attention. Although he may do his best to share things with other toddlers in his playgroup, it is much harder for him. Eventually he succeeds, but the fact that he enjoyed a solitary existence during his most formative years may well leave its mark on his personality for the rest of his life. Only children never seem to suffer from loneliness as adults. They positively relish solitude and, although they may learn to become highly sociable, they are still likely to spend some time on their own.

the oldest child

The first-born who has younger siblings gains a double advantage over other infants. For the first year or two of his life he enjoys the full attention of his new parents and is treated royally as an only child. He learns how much he is loved without any interruptions or interference. His ego blossoms and he rates himself as being "worthy of love." But then, before he has the chance to become swollen-headed, along comes baby number two and suddenly he finds that almost all of the parental attention is now focused on this tiny new arrival. He has to come to terms with this, but when he does so, he does not lose his own sense of self-worth. This means that he has a solid foundation of "self" on which he can now build the limiting factors of social sharing. The result is a self-assured personality that is capable of a genuine mixing-in with others.

the younger child

The baby born into a home in which there are small children already is surrounded by stronger, competing siblings from the first day. Whether he is the second, third or fourth child makes comparatively little difference. In all such cases there is always an older child looming above him. These children tend to grow up to become highly sociable individuals but often without quite the sense of personal identity and importance that one finds in only children or in the first-born. When a younger child reaches the toddler stage he frequently has to take second place, and quickly learns that all toys are not intended solely for him. Even those toys designated as his may find their way into the arms of an older sibling, with predictable results. One special advantage he does has, however, is that, as the "baby" of the family, he may find that, if threatened by outsiders, his older siblings will come to his rescue.

relating to other children

When a baby meets another child for the first time, the strange infant is just another intriguing object to be explored, like any feature of her surroundings. She makes little distinction between the other baby and, say, a large soft toy or a talking doll. She may reach out to prod her new companion, investigating her to find out more, but there is no empathy and no understanding that this is a being like herself. True social interaction does not happen until much later, at the playgroup stage.

Play activities at the baby stage of life are typically solitary, with companions treated largely as "toys." There may be some degree of imitation, when two babies who are sitting near one another engage in parallel play, but this is not true cooperative, social interaction. Parents who notice two babies sitting together and smiling at one another might imagine that they are witnessing an exchange of body language that, in older children and adults, would be a friendly greeting. But at this very early stage, a smile is more likely to be an independent action reflecting the amusement a baby feels at the sight of a fascinating object. If a baby starts to cry her companion may become upset, but this is more likely to be distress caused by an unpleasant sound rather than a sign of sympathy.

Incidentally, a baby reacts to pet animals in the same way, poking a dog or a cat as she would another baby. For this reason, pets are better introduced when the child is much older and can share responsibility for caring for them. A baby should never be left unsupervised with a family pet.

becoming independent

growing confidence

Approaching his second birthday, a toddler stands on the threshold of a time of great wonder and excitement. He still has three years before school starts in earnest, and during this time he is at his most enchanted and enchanting. Given half the chance, he enjoys every day to the fullest as he joyfully explores new levels of language, new muscular skills and new mental challenges. With the helpless stage of babyhood fading into the past, and the serious stage of cultural training still way off in the future, he can wake up every morning with high hopes of having some serious fun and enjoying what may well be the most innocent and happiest days of his entire life.

feelings of insecurity

At around this time, a toddler starts talking to and meeting other children. A child who has been introduced to a variety of situations and who is used to meeting other people from a young age will develop trust and the ability to cope with new experiences. With some children this process is a smooth, gradual one without any major upsets or traumas. With others, however, there are moments of panic and acute distress, with the infant unable to break away from parental protection when expected to do so.

the moment of separation

Infants can be very wary of being left alone with strangers. Even at the age of two, the child may keep one eye on the parent who took them to a playgroup, in case she suddenly disappears. There is a temptation for an adult to wait for her toddler to become engrossed in some game with an exciting new toy and then sneak away when he is not looking. Once this stratagem has been discovered it may appear to the toddler that he has been abandoned, and a panic response may then erupt that it is difficult to control. It makes better sense in the young one's mind if the parent says goodbye with a hug and a kiss and a reassurance that she will soon return to collect him. There may be a moment of crying or panic, but this usually dies down following a swift parental exit and some fascinating diversion created by the playgroup organizer. A short spell of crying is a sign that the child has formed a secure attachment with his parents, not that he is truly insecure.

confidence boosters

There are various ways in which a parent can boost a toddler's confidence. Obviously, offering comfort, love and support at times of distress is one of them. Another is to "let go": allowing a toddler to explore his environment by and for himself is paramount, as long as that environment is safe. In this way, he adds to his experiences and learns to face new challenges head on, finding solutions to problems on his own. Knowing a parent is close at hand encourages him to do this more readily and is an early indication of his emerging independence.

the confident child

The more secure a baby feels in the early stages of life, and the more he trusts his parents, the more self-confident he becomes. His parents prove to him that he is lovable and he therefore develops a sense of self-worth and feels at ease with himself – something he builds on as a toddler. He becomes the one who makes the first moves toward more independent actions. His parents do not have to push him. Instead, he takes the lead, and slowly but surely starts to express himself as a self-confident, outgoing individual, ready to assert himself and accept new challenges.

a busy age

Much has been written about the difficult behavior of the increasingly independent two-year-old, and the phrase "the terrible twos" has been coined to describe this particular phase of childhood. Indeed, this especially challenging time for parents abounds with stories of memorable moments in the lives of toddlers, and how they shock and shame the adults with whom they come into contact.

Close examination of such incidents, however, reveals that most of these children are charming rather than annoying, amusing rather than irritating. Many of the tales recounted hardly justify the term "terrible twos." It is true that toddlers go through a somewhat eccentric phase at this age, asserting their independence often beyond their ability. But, despite the occasional stubborn refusal or temper tantrum, the days of the two-year-old are full of delightful surprises, both for the toddler and for the parents.

always on the go

Children of this age are well equipped with good memory, unlimited energy and an intense curiosity. They exhibit a cheerful playfulness that seems to last from breakfast to bedtime, and which can exhaust even the most loving of parents. Having finally acquired the physical and mental equipment with which to explore the world, the two-year-old is simply impatient to get going. There is so much to be done, and so much to learn. Difficulties only arise if, for some reason, there is too little to do. If, one day, for some special reason, she must be patient and stay still, frustration may quickly surface and the toddler can easily become restless and irritable.

a safe space

Toddlers love exploring their surroundings and their intense curiosity can make them accident prone. However, studies have found that they prefer not to venture too far from the parental protector. One investigation that recorded the behavior of toddlers in parks found that, with a few exceptions, the children did not stray beyond 200 feet (60 m) of their mothers. This radius matched what the parent considered to be a safe distance.

interacting with the world

The two-year-old arrives at the stage where she not only has a modest vocabulary, but also loves to chatter, trying out new ways of combining and recombining her words. Her amazing brain, genetically programmed for the rapid acquisition of verbal language, is at the start of a magical period of development characterized by an insatiable urge to conquer grammar, expand vocabulary and improve on word pronunciation.

an organic process

None of this involves formal lessons or analytical thinking. It just happens, and is wonderful to watch. What is more, the two-year-old takes a special pleasure in the fact that she impresses her parents. They perceive something new in her almost every day and, if there is a happy family atmosphere, their delight in her progress makes it blossom even more.

a healthy imagination

A toddler's imagination begins to flourish at this stage, with the two-year-old engaging in amusing pretend play with toys, and starting to enjoy that most human of preoccupations – exploring the world of fantasy. Almost all of her activities involve some form of play and she relishes games in which she can act out everyday scenes she sees around her. Given toy animals or dolls to play with, she chatters away, creating simple scenes. She happily combines her worlds of fantasy and reality – for her there is no need to distinguish between them – and everyday events merge with pretend ones. As a result, many children from the age of two to five invent one or more imaginary friends with whom to share their daily experiences.

parental lessons

It is interesting how often a toddler chooses to act out the role of a parent in her fantasy play, scolding a toy character for behaving badly, or praising it for doing something well. This reveals the extent to which, even at an early age, a toddler remembers the precise way in which she has been treated by her mother and father. Even such small details as a wagging forefinger or a frowning brow will be reproduced when she is disciplining a "misbehaving" toy or wayward doll.

interpreting the world

A two-year-old will listen with interest to the conversations going on around her. She loves asking questions and is increasingly able to understand the explanations. She now begins to remember past events, and to delight in recounting them. However, her attempts to make sense of the world can lead to misunderstandings and even some irrational fears. A child who sees a toy swept down the drain with the bath water may be scared, the next time she has a bath, that she will go the same way herself!

toilet training

All parents look forward to the moment when their toddler becomes toilet trained and it is at last possible to abandon the tiresome routine of changing soiled garments. However, this is a process that is impossible to rush and the rate of success depends mostly on waiting until the toddler's nervous system is sufficiently developed for him to sense when his bowel and bladder are full (see Dealing with waste, page 98).

toilet timing

During his first year of life a baby defecates automatically when he senses an increased pressure in his bowels. This is a reflex action and beyond any sort of deliberate control. In other words, a very young baby cannot be toilet trained, regardless of any efforts made by hygiene-conscious, over-zealous parents. Yet, despite this, it has been reported that in some countries as many as 80 percent of babies are subjected to repeated attempts by their parents to impose toilet discipline on them during this early phase. Furthermore, some parents proudly proclaim that they have been successful, even though human biology indicates that this is impossible. So what is happening in these cases?

The answer is "toilet timing" as distinct from true "toilet training." A mother notices that her baby is most likely to defecate shortly after a meal, so she develops a routine of placing him on a potty immediately after feeding him. This may well catch the moment when evacuation occurs but the baby is not actively cooperating since defecation is still no more than a reflex action. Even if the mother praises her baby and the baby senses that his mother is pleased with him, he cannot consciously control this action.

signs of readiness

Once a baby has passed his first birthday, he is at last able to control his bodily functions, although this does not happen overnight. Girls usually achieve this stage before boys and toddlers are generally clean before they are dry, but there are no hard-and-fast rules. Typically, it takes some months for the voluntary control of the sphincter muscle to fully develop. The youngest age at which this can happen is between 12 and 15 months, but 18 months is more usual and some infants take much longer. As so often happens with childhood development, there is considerable individual variation and there is no need for concern if some toddlers are late starters.

A toddler may show that he is about to pass a bowel motion by screwing up his face or crouching down. Toddlers are often fascinated by what they have excreted and may even pick up and proudly offer the contents of their potty as a present since they have yet to learn disgust. Others are intimidated by the whole process and require lots of praise and reassurance.

acting for oneself

When a toddler reaches the age of two, a new trend begins to surface more and more. She starts to insist on doing things for herself. Where, in earlier months, the infant was only too glad to be dressed, fed, picked up and carried by her parents, she now starts to resist help and tries to perform these actions herself.

dressing

A small baby offers no assistance when dressed by a parent. She enjoys the process because it means intimate body contact, but she can do little to help. Then, at about the age of one year, she starts to hold out an arm or a leg to assist with the dressing procedure. A few months later she may show the first signs of self-dressing, usually in the form of pulling on her socks. At 18 months she may try putting on her shoes as well as her socks – but there is only a 50/50 chance that they end up on the correct feet. She may also, at this age, struggle to take off her clothes at bedtime.

At the age of two years, there comes a morning when, much to the mother's surprise, the toddler appears fully dressed and delighted by the warm reception she gets for this feat. The clothes she is wearing may be an odd mixture, but she is very proud of having "won" this particular game. Unfortunately, a game is precisely what it is to her, rather than a daily routine. So the following day may find her back where she was, waiting for her mother to dress her. It was the novelty of dressing herself for the first time that mattered and that thrill has now gone. Another year or so may pass before she is truly and regularly self-dressing.

let me do it!

A two-year-old carries this trend of "do it myself" into all areas of her life – dressing, feeding, playing – and frequently resists parental attempts to help. She is not too upset by a tentative offer of help, but a more forceful insistence may cause an angry refusal because, in the child's mind, this is insulting. The parent must become a diplomat, adept at letting the child think that she has decided to do something in a particular way, and always ready with a distraction strategy when things start to go badly wrong.

making choices

Along with a ready desire to do everything for herself, comes a toddler's wish to shift from the passive acceptance of choices made by her parents, to choosing things for herself. This makes life more complicated, but it also makes it more interesting and it helps to pave the way for an increasingly independent existence.

A good example of this is when it comes to eating and a toddler starts to refuse certain foods. To the parent, repeated food refusals gradually become more and more irritating, but to the infant they provide an entertaining new game. And this is just the beginning of "choosing games." Any situation in which the toddler's changing preferences can prolong an interaction with a parent is an opportunity, both for more attention from the parent and for striking a tiny blow for her newly emerging sense of independence.

a positive outlook

In addition to feeding, the two-year-old may express her independence in other contexts, such as clothes, games, walks and sleeping arrangements. Parents always win in the end, but bullying is the worst way of approaching this problem. It helps to view the tiny child in these rebellious situations as displaying bravery rather than hostility. It must take an enormous effort for the toddler to set herself up against the power of the adult world and, no matter how annoying certain actions may be, these actions are clear signs of a growing strength of character that slowly move the child toward a fully independent existence. This whole process may take two whole decades, but with the choosy two-year-old we see the very first signs of the beginning of this long journey.

getting along with others

A two-year-old is on the threshold of a vital new kind of experience – sharing with other children. This idea may take a while to catch on, but fortunately humans happen to be programmed as highly cooperative beings, and eventually the concept of helping one another takes root.

learning to share

Sharing can take place in the home when other toddlers come to visit, but there is a difficulty with this scenario, since the home toddler and the visiting toddler have unequal status. All the toys inevitably belong to the home toddler and the visitor must tread carefully. Two-year-old children still have a strong egocentric view of life and they think of everything in terms of "mine." They don't understand that a shared toy will eventually be returned to them, and conflicts may ensue.

the playgroup

A much better environment for learning about sharing is the playgroup. Here every toddler enjoys the same status, and there are no parents to interfere and show favor to their own (or, worse still, someone else's) child. For some, attending a playgroup can prove rather daunting, while others take to it very quickly, excited by the novelties offered there. These novelties are not just a matter of new toys, but also of new friends and playing in groups. Little by little the concepts of sharing, watching and taking turns sink in, until eventually the joy of group games is discovered. Admittedly, for the two-year-old these developments are only at their very beginning, but even a limited experience of social interaction with young strangers, who soon become familiar friends, helps to sow the seeds from which grows an increasing ability to deal with separation from parental protection.

new friends

Once playgroup attendance becomes a matter of routine, and the initial separation anxieties are forgotten, it soon develops into a crucial social learning experience. In a tribal society, all this would happen smoothly and imperceptibly because there would be toddlers running free all over the settlement, watched over by all the nearby adults. In that primeval situation there was no need of special locations for playgroups, or of taking toddlers to timed appointments. But our modern way of life tends to shut each family away from all others in separate apartments or houses. This is unnatural for the human species, but it is an aspect of civilization that we cannot ignore.

As adults, we learn to adapt and to organize social gatherings to prevent too much isolation, but for our infants it is a different matter. It is all too easy for young children to become so embedded in the family home that they hardly know how to deal with the outside world. The result of this can be seen outside any school building on the child's first day of serious schooling. While some march happily through the door, others hang back miserably and refuse to leave their parents. Even at the much later age of five, the ghosts of separation anxiety still haunt them. This is why repeated early exposure to playgroups and to children who are not members of the close family is so helpful in laying the foundations for a child's later social independence.

the future

Looking into the tiny face of a newborn baby as she nestles in her mother's arms, it is important to remember that the way the little infant is treated during the first two years of her life will have a profound effect upon the course she takes later as an adult. It should be easy enough for a child who has enjoyed a loving, richly stimulating, fun-packed infancy to grow up into a happy, well-adjusted adult. For an neglected or deprived infant, however, it may prove much harder.

There is evidence to support this view from studies of those individuals who have failed to adapt to adult life. Investigations of inmates in European prisons have revealed that no fewer than 50 percent of them were subjected to more than five changes in their mother-figure during their childhood. A staggering 95 percent of them said that they had never enjoyed the loving care of a single mother-figure. Instead, a confusing mixture of different individuals had looked after them.

So the kind of antisocial person who ends up in jail is much more likely to have been deprived of the intense childhood bonding experience, when compared with members of the human population at large. Some modern theories, which claim that loving mothers are not as important to their babies as traditional beliefs suggest, collapse in the face of this kind of evidence. Clearly, the first two years of life are deeply formative and therefore crucially important. In an ideal world, those first two years should be the most

idyllic of all. From feeding contentedly in her mother's arms and cuddling up in the warm embrace of her body, to exploring the exciting world of toys and games and feeling the thrill of growing confidence as she slowly acquires mobility and self-control, every baby should have the opportunity to enjoy a prelude to life that is gloriously satisfying and increasingly stimulating.

Anyone, whether a parent or not, who takes a close look at the amazing journey undertaken by the human infant as she grows from a minute fertilized egg to a lively, enchanting two-year-old, can only marvel at the incredible complexity of the developing human being – the most extraordinary form of life ever to take breath on our planet. And it is not exaggerating to say that the future of humanity lies in the hands of those whose loving care ensures that the next generation of babies will thrive in an environment that encourages their astonishing natural qualities to unfold and to blossom.

index

acknowledgments

author's acknowledgments

I would like express my enormous debt to my wife Ramona for her tireless research that kept me up to date with all the latest reports on this fascinating subject. And a special thanks to my grandchildren for once again bringing me face to face with the reality of what it is to be experiencing the first two years of life on this exciting planet.

My thanks also to Jane McIntosh of Hamlyn, Fiona Robertson and Anna Southgate for their extensive and painstaking editorial work on this book. I would also like to acknowledge the splendid contribution of Karen Sawyer and Janis Utton, whose wonderful visual designs have made this volume such a feast for the eyes. And finally, my thanks to my literary agent, Silke Bruenink, for her expert help in setting up this project.

picture acknowledgments

1 Getty Images/Jade Albert Studio, Inc; 2 Getty Images/Maria Taglienti; 4 above Jupiter Images/Rubberball/Nicole Hill, below Masterfile/Kathleen Finlay; 5 above Masterfile/Scott Tysick, below Corbis/Pixland; 7 Masterfile/Michele/Salmieri; 9 Getty Images/Patricia Doyle; 10 Getty Images/Jay Reilly; 13 above left Getty Images/Time Life/Bill Ray, above right Masterfile/David Muir, below left Getty Images/Lisa Spindler Photography Inc, below right Jupiter Images/Creatas/Adrian Peacock; 14 istockphoto.com/Jill Lang; 15 Masterfile/Keate; 17 Photolibrary Group /Mauritius Images/Simon Katzer; 19 SuperStock/Francisco Cruz; 21 above left Photolibrary Group/Mauritius/Marina Raith; above right Alamy/Profimedia International sro; below left Mother and Baby Picture Library/Ian Hooton; below right Masterfile/Kathleen Finlay; 22 Getty Images/Jim Cummins; 24 Photolibrary Group/Picture Press/B Koenig; 25 Corbis/Zefa/Larry Williams; 26 Getty Images/Zac Macauley; 28 Photolibrary Group/Mauritius/Reik Reik; 30 SuperStock/maXx images; 33 Getty Images/Juan Silva; 34 Alamy/Picture Partners; 36 Getty Images/Steve Allen; 37 Photolibrary Group/Folio/Nina Ramsby; 39 Alamy/Chris Stock Photography, inset above Getty Images/Dr David Phillips/Visuals Unlimited, inset below Science Photo Library/Steve Gschmeissner; 40 Getty Images/DK Stock/Kristin I Stith; 43 Corbis/Digital Art, inset Corbis/Tim Pannell; 44–45 Babystock.com/Penny Gentieu; 47 above left Getty Images, above right Imagestate/First Light, below left Jupiter Images/TongRo Image Stock, below right Jupiter Images/Constance Bannister; 49 Babystock.com/Penny Gentieu, inset Science Photo Library; 50 above left Masterfile/Ron Fehling, above right Getty Images/Victoria Blackie, below left Getty Images/Altrendo Images, below right Corbis/Bloomimage; 53 Getty Images/Johner Images; 55 above left Getty Images/Benelux Press, above right Corbis/Jamie Grill, below left Getty Images/Queerstock, below right Photolibrary Group/Index Stock Imagery/Parker Jacque Denzer; 56 Getty Images/Jamie Grill; 57 Jupiter Images/Banana Stock; 59 above left Getty Images/Tim Flach, below left Photolibrary Group/Ron Seymour, right Getty Images/Michael Orton; 60 Photolibrary Group/Jerry Driendl; 62, 63 Photolibrary Group/American Inc; 65 Corbis/Larry Williams; 66 Getty Images/Sharon Montrose; 69 above left Science Photo Library/GustoImages, above right Science Photo Library/Ian Boddy, below left Getty Images/Jim Pickerell, below right Getty Images/Roger Wright; 71 Jupiter Images/ Asia Images/Marcus Mok; 72 Tina Bolton; 74–75 Alamy/Profimedia International sro/Peter Banos; 77 Corbis/Jim Craigmyle; 78 left & right Jupiter Images/Babystock/Penny Gentieu; 79 left & right Babystock.com/Penny Gentieu; 80 Getty Images/Eric Schnakenberg; 82 Getty Images/Digital Vision; 85 Science Photo Library/Cristina Pedrazzini; 86 Getty Images/Barbara Peacock; 87 Getty Images/Lisa Spindler Photography Inc; 89 all Photolibrary Group/Picture Press/Sandra Seckinger; 90 Getty Images/Maria Taglienti; 93 Getty Images/Camille Tokerud; 94 Getty Images/Charly Franklin; 97 Getty Images/Rubberball, inset Science Photo Library/Eye of Science; 98 Photolibrary Group/PhotoAlto/Frederic Cirou; 99 Science Photo Library; 101 above left Getty Images/Ed Fox, above right Masterfile/Royalty Free, below left Alamy/Profimedia International sro, below right Alamy/Gary Roebuck; 102 Getty Images/Jade Albert Studio, Inc; 104 Corbis/Larry Williams; 106 above & below left Jupiter Images/Babystock/Penny Gentieu, above & below right Babystock.com/Penny Gentieu; 109 Masterfile/Michele/Salmieri; 110 Getty Images/Mel Yates; 113 Masterfile/Bob Anderson; 114 above left Getty Images/Ghislain & Marie David de Lossy, 114 above right Corbis/Jamie Grill, below left Getty Images/Altrendo Images, below right Corbis/Larry Williams; 117 Corbis/Joyce Choo; 118 Corbis/Pixland; 120 left & right Tatjana Alvegard Photographie; 121 left & right Punchstock/Upper Cut/Tatjana Alvegard; 122 Getty Images/Hitoshi Nishimura; 124 Photolibrary Group/Digital Vision; 127 SuperStock/age fotostock; 129 Octopus Publishing Group/Russell Sadur; 131 Photolibrary Group/Blend Images/Ariel Skelley; 132 Alamy/Picture Partners; 134 Getty Images Altrendo Images; 137 above left Getty Images/Iconica/Clive Shalice, above right Photolibrary Group/Picture Press/Julia Kruger, below left Photolibrary Group/LWA/Dann Tardiff, below right Jupiter Images/Creatas; 138 Alamy/Picture Partners; 141 Getty Images/Michele/Salmieri; 142 Jupiter Images/Fancy/Heide Benser; 143 Alamy/Jupiter Images/Creatas; 145 Getty Images/Michel Tcherevkoff; 146, 149 above & below Punchstock/Digital Vision/Alistair Berg; 151 Getty Images/Lisa Spindler Photography Inc; 152 Jupiter Images/Babystock/Penny Gentieu; 154, 155 Corbis/Larry Williams; 157 above left Corbis/Chris Coxwell, above right & below Corbis/Lawrence Manning; 159 Getty Images/Barbara Peacock; 160 SuperStock/Sampson Williams; 161 Photolibrary Group/Folio/Katja Halvarsson; 163 above left Science Photo Library/Ian Boddy, above right Corbis/Nick North, below left Shutterstock/rickt, below right Getty Images/Karan Kapoor; 164 Getty Images/Elyse Lewin; 167 above left Photolibrary Group/Design Pics Inc, above right Alamy/The Photolibrary Wales, below left Alamy/PhotoAlto/ Laurence Mouton, below right Getty Images/Ian Boddy; 168 Photolibrary Group/Folio/Lukas Deurloo; 170 Punchstock/Digital Vision; 172 Getty Images/Christopher Robbins; 175 Photolibrary Group/PhotoAlto/Rafal Strzechwski; 176 Photolibrary Group/Banana Stock; 177 Getty Images/Lisa Spindler Photography Inc; 179 Mother and Baby Picture Library/Paul Mitchell; 181 Getty Images/Altrendo Images; 182 Corbis/Nick North; 185 all Masterfile/Marko MacPherson; 187 above & below Alamy/Blend Images/David Buffington.